MW01264398

The Fear of Man vs. The Fear of God

How to Get Out of the Wilderness Into the Promised Land

By
Philip DelRe

Voice Publishing USA

The Fear of Man vs. The Fear of God
How to Get Out of the Wilderness Into the Promised Land

Philip DelRe

© Copyright 2010 by Voice Publishing
A Division of Voice in the Wilderness Ministries
Belvidere, IL 61008 USA

ISBN 978-0-9677520-6-8

Printed in the United States of America.

Please visit our website for other helpful resources: www.voice-wilderness.org

For information regarding speaking engagements, please contact:
Voice in the Wilderness Ministries at (815) 547-0765.

What people are saying about the man, the ministry, and the materials . . .

"Philip DelRe has excelled in bringing together powerful thoughts on a most important theme."

Ray Comfort
Host of *The Way of the Master* TV series with Kirk Cameron, evangelist, author, and speaker

"Phil DelRe powerfully communicates the Gospel and overflows with a passion to reach the lost."

Dr. Robert Coleman
Author of the best-selling *The Master Plan of Evangelism.* Former Dean of the Billy Graham International School of Evangelism and currently a professor at Gordon-Conwell Theological Seminary

"Phil DelRe's tract: *God's Three Witnesses* is the finest Gospel tract I have ever seen." His book, *"The Fear of Man Vs. The Fear Of God"* touched my heart. It really is a clarion call to action."

Dr. David Larsen
Professor of Preaching Emeritus at Trinity Evangelical Divinity School and author of 18 books, including the 900 page, *History of Preaching,* published by Kregel

"In an era of fadism and fashionable substitutes for true scriptural principles the ministry of Phil DelRe is a ray of hope for the church. Phil has tapped into the mode of true Gospel evangelism that has proved so mighty in the past. For anyone desirous of seeing the type of deep and through heart work that so characterized the church in better days, Phil should not only be heard but studied."

Reddit Andrews
Director of Chapel, Trinity International University

"In a fear-filled world, Philip DelRe has written a compelling manual to guide us to God's peace, wisdom, security, and the abundant life worth living. He maps it out so strategically that we can die for the cause and celebrate through all eternity that it was the best of all ways to live.

"*In The Fear of Man Vs. The Fear Of God*, Phil's message is clear for all of us who want to be well-anchored in God and to serve His great redemptive cause. Read it! Be strengthened; be more focused, and ready to make your God-sized mark. This is a must-read!"

Dr. Bob Griffin
President, Rockford Renewal Ministries Author: *Firestorms of Revival; How Historic Moves of God Happened and Will Happen Again*, Creation House

"Phil's message is right from the Father heart of God."

Ray Sanders
Director of Christian Friends of Israel

"It's a terrific message—and I can understand listening to it why it had such power. You're quite right in saying it's nothing more than the word of God, but you, of course, presented it very effectively and made the case very powerfully."

Chuck Colson
Chairman and Founder of Prison Fellowship

"That was the clearest and most complete evangelistic message I have ever heard. I doubt that there was a hard heart left in the room. You need to get this published so the whole world can read it."

Todd Wendorf
Associate Pastor at Saddleback Community Church

"I have been attending seminars for over 40 years, and your presentation was the most direct presentation of the Gospel I have heard."

Pastor attending the *Beyond Amsterdam 2000* Conference
Sponsored by the Billy Graham Evangelistic Association and the Evangelical Fellowship of Zambia

Phil DelRe is a *no-fear* apologist with a sense of humor. His anecdotal style helps the medicine go down and accompanies a sense of urgency to embolden believers. His new book *The Fear of Man vs. The Fear of God* is a good read and a great resource for study groups.

Fred Tscholl
Manager, WFEN Radio

Without a doubt Philip DelRe is anointed. When Philip came to our church he spoke on *The Fear of Man*. The response was tremendous. The Holy Spirit dealt deeply with our hearts and the altar call lasted well over 30 minutes—not by manipulation but by genuine conviction. Philip DelRe and Voice in the Wilderness Ministries are unique, relevant and timely.

Todd Greiner
Senior pastor of Community of Faith Church for over 20 years
and founder of Church Without Walls in Southern Illinois.

"Phil DelRe is a Ten Commandments scholar."

Bob Cornuke
International adventurer and explorer Author of: *In Search of the Mountain of God. The Discovery of the Real Mt. Sinai.*

"I absolutely love your book, *God the Final Frontier*. I want my whole family to read it. Your facts on the universe and the Trinity were fascinating!"

Debra Moffett
Co-host of the Harvest Show and Miss America 1983

"Your message on law and grace was the most fantastic, fantastic, fantastic sermon we've ever heard in our life."

Tim & Sarah Brown
Students, Trinity International Divinity School

"The cause of Christ is too often impeded by the fear of man, and Phil Del Re is out to change all that. He's the perfect teacher on this subject, for he truly fears God and not people. In this important work, he shows us how to be delivered from the fear of man. Read it and prepare to slay giants."

Roger Knowlton
Senior Pastor of Edgewood Community Church, Waupon Wisconsin

"Last spring I heard you speak in the undergraduate chapel at Moody. After your message I picked up a tape, and I have listened to that tape at least twenty times. That was the first day I ever heard such a clear explanation of the Gospel in such a Biblical way."

David Lieske
M. Div. Student, Moody Bible Institute

"I just read your booklet on Jehovah's Witnesses. It is the best resource I have found to refute their false doctrine. I have never seen anything worded better. Your argument is indisputable."

Dominic Digangi
Former national speaker for the Jehovah's Witnesses

Table of Contents

Introduction

One of God's greatest promises to man (in this life) is found in Deuteronomy chapter 28. God promised the Israelites: if they would love, trust, and obey Him, in His sovereign power, He would exalt them far above all the other nations. Spiritually, intellectually, economically, militarily, and politically they would stand alone as the greatest and most powerful nation on earth.

If, on the other hand they rebelled, if they failed to do what they were chosen to do, God would allow the curse of sin to run its course on the nation. Either way, the sovereign power and divine nature of the invisible God would be clearly revealed to the nations through Israel; whether the blessing or the curse, the choice was theirs (see Deut. 28 and Lev. 26).

In 1 Cor. 10:1-12, in the New Testament, God says the same principle applies to the church today. God is saying, if we get our priorities right, if we love the God who created the world, more than the things He created, then, He will glorify Himself by blessing His people with abundant life.

The problem is we love the praise of man more than the praise that comes from the only God. Stated negatively, Prv. 29:25 says:

> "The fear of man brings a snare, But he who trusts in the Lord will be exalted."

The fear of man is idolatry which is spiritual adultery. God cannot bless unfaithfulness. Just as the Israelites failed to take the Promised Land because of the fear of man, so the church has fallen to the same deception.

The Bible has a lot to say about the fear of man vs. the fear of God. This book is a clarion call for Christians to come out of the closet, and into the Promised Land that flows with milk and honey. The choice is yours!

CHAPTER ONE

"The Christians Are Here; Call Out The Lions!"

—◊◊◊—

It was a beautiful Thursday night in Chicago just before 7 p.m. I was walking into the "Super Maximum Security" division of the Cook County jail—one of the most notorious county jails in the United States. As a chaplain, I have been preaching there once, twice, and sometimes three times a week for the last 18 years. It's an absolutely incredible place. On 96 acres, it's the largest county jail in America. It's a city within a city. There are 10,000 men and 1,500 women locked up behind hundreds of thousands of tons of cement and steel. As many as 100,000 men and women will be processed through the jail each year. It has an underground tunnel system connecting 10 of the 11 divisions. It has almost 4,000 full-time employees, and its own hospital. When the first division was constructed in 1929, it included a small room with one piece of furniture—the electric chair; they call it the "Ice House." In 1931 Al Capone became one of its most notorious inmates. In 1971, blues legend B.B. King recorded an album there appropriately titled: *B. B. King—Live at Cook County Jail.* And, in 1996, the *Back to God Hour* produced a television special there entitled: *Back to the Streets.*[1] It featured *our* ministry.

Super-Maximum Security

"Super max" is where they keep the highest-bond and no-bond inmates. Here you will find the most violent men charged with the most heinous crimes. Division 11 is also the newest addition to the jail. At a construction cost of more than $100 million, it's huge, it's all white, and I call it the Taj Mahal. Each block is air conditioned, and furnished with a colored TV. Every inmate gets "three hots and a cot," and the best police protection money can buy. Ironically, they also get a piece of cake or a cookie on their dinner trays!

Once inside, I take the elevator up to the third floor to the security office in order to sign in and pick up my I.D. badge. Security officers will then arrange to have the men escorted to the chapel. On special occasions, we have had as many as 1,200 inmates in the gymnasium for chapel! Exiting the elevator and approaching the security office, I spy an officer sitting at his desk I have not seen for some time. That's because they are transferred from division to division every year or so just to "shake things up." I have known this particular officer for the last 18 years, and every time I run into him (he's like a Mack truck) he's taken every opportunity to insult me personally, to mock Christianity, and to openly mock God! I have met some characters over the years as you might imagine, but this man is in a class by himself.

As I'm approaching the security office, he sees me and I see him. As I walk in, he stands up and assumes the stance of a weight lifter about to try out for the world's record. You know, leaning slightly forward, arms hanging down slightly curled in, flexing his muscles; sort of like a turkey spreading its wings to show off. In a loud voice, with his eyes fixed on me, he barks at the two officers across the room:

"THE CHRISTIANS ARE HERE; CALL OUT THE LIONS!"

Without hesitation, but rather sheepishly at first, I replied, "Sergeant, I'd like to remind you that it was 2,000 years ago that the Roman Empire was feeding Christians to the lions, and we have the incredible perspective of being able to look back over 2,000 years of recorded history and what do we see?" Getting louder and bolder I said, "There are more Christians alive at this moment than the total number of people that made up the Roman Empire over its entire 500-year history,

AND THE LIONS AND TIGERS ARE ON THE
ENDANGERED-SPECIES LIST. WE'RE NOT
AFRAID OF LIONS; BRING 'EM ON!"

I looked at him, and his jaw dropped. I looked at the two officers in the corner, and their mouths were open so wide they could have eaten a banana sideways! The sergeant, slightly discombobulated, broke the silence and ordered the officers, "Call chapel!" So, what is the point of this story? Simply this:

When You're Right About God, And You're Right With God, You Never Have To Be Intimidated By The World, The Flesh, Or The Devil Himself. And, It's Okay To Get Excited About Jesus!

As an interesting follow-up to that story, that officer is now my best friend at the jail. He actually goes out of his way to help us bring more men to chapel. Best of all, he now asks me questions about the Bible!

The Fear Of Man

The Bible has a lot to say about the fear of man vs. the fear of God. It should be ruled a "no contest," but unfortunately not everybody sees it that way. It appears most people, including many who claim to be "Christians," are more concerned with what people think than what God thinks. My hope is that this book will serve as a clarion call for Christians to come out of the closet and get real with God.

Humanly speaking, our problem is understandable since we see men but we have never seen God. However, that rationale becomes irrational when we realize that man could not have created the universe. Only an all-powerful and eternal being could do that. When life is over we are accountable to the Eternal God, not to mortal man. What will we be held accountable for? We will be held accountable for what we did with our time, our talent, our treasure, and our temple.

As ambassadors for Christ, Christians have been entrusted with the ministry of reconciliation (2 Cor. 5:18-21). Sin has separated man from his Creator, and the church has been given the unspeakable privilege and great responsibility of sharing the good news that Jesus paid the penalty for sin once and for all. The world has no hope apart from God's salvation in Christ. Man will never solve his own problems because man *is* the problem.

Christ alone answers the most profound questions beating in the human heart; namely, who am I? Where did I come from? Why am I here? Where am I going? What is the meaning of life? How can I be free from the guilt and the power of sin?

Sharing the truth about Jesus Christ with others is called evangelism. Unfortunately, statistics show that 95% of people who claim to be "Evangelical Christians" have never even attempted to lead another person to faith in Christ. Why, if we really believe the Bible to be true, do we remain silent? What kind of human being would you be if you had the cure for cancer or AIDS, but refused to share it with the world?

I am convinced, based on Scripture and experience that the number-one reason people refuse to learn how to present the Gospel is because of the fear of man. Curiously, many unbelievers have no qualms about mocking Christians, but many Christians are afraid to engage unbelievers concerning their need for salvation in Jesus Christ. Children of light should never be intimidated by children of darkness. It is in this context that a great preacher from the past once said:

> "As the profane take the liberty to force their irreligion upon you, so you take the liberty to force your religion upon them." C.H. Spurgeon

Spurgeon was not suggesting that we try to "shove religion down peoples' throats." He knew that was not possible. He was saying that we, as stewards of truth, should be as bold and outspoken about our beliefs as the pagans are about theirs. After all, we're right!

The Gun That Kills Without Bullets

The most common form the fear of man takes is purely psychological. It's like a gun without bullets. You can control people with a gun, even if it's not loaded—as long as they are unaware of it. In reality, its power is all in their mind. If they discover that the gun has no ammunition, the game is over.

Like a coin, the fear of man has two sides, the positive and the negative. We call it *peer pressure*. On one side we have the fear of what people will think of us. On the reverse side, we love the praise of men. Both the fear and the love of what people think are rooted in one and the same thing—pride. We are more affected by this spiritual disease than most of us realize.

For many of us, the most important decisions we make in life are based not on what is best or most practical, but on what other people will think, say, or do. Everything from the car we drive to the shoes we wear is motivated in whole or in part by how we think we will be perceived by other people. This is the driving force behind materialism.

The average family in America is enslaved by credit-card debt. These cards should be called "covet cards." We buy things we don't need, with money we don't have, to impress people we don't even like. We need to get real. In Luke 16:15, Jesus said:

> "...You are those who justify yourselves before men, but God knows your hearts. For what is highly esteemed among men is an abomination in the sight of God."

In John 5:44, Jesus asks:

> "How can you believe, when you receive glory from one another, and you do not seek the glory that is from the one and only God?"

Another reason that the fear of man is so prevalent is this: Many people are psychologically oriented rather than truth-oriented. They live by feelings rather than facts. You can be wrong about a lot of things, but if you are wrong about who Jesus Christ is, and what it means to believe in Him, you are wrong enough to be separated from God forever!

According to psychologists, three major factors motivate most people. They are: (1) the desire for gain, (2) the fear of loss, and (3) the need to love and be loved. These three things either work for you or against you; it all depends on whether you are living for time or eternity.

The Desire For Gain And The Fear Of Loss

If you knew a financial investment that was increasing 100% per year, would you tell all your friends about it, even though some of them might not believe you? What if it was increasing 10,000% a year? Would that excite you enough to share it with your friends? Take a look at this investment from Mark 4:20:

> "And those are the ones on whom seed was sown on the good soil; and they hear the word and accept it, and bear fruit, thirty, sixty, and a hundredfold."

The "seed" in this verse speaks of evangelism. The hundredfold return is not 100%; that would simply be a one-fold return. A hundredfold return is 10,000%. Do the math on that. If you invest $1,000 and get a 10,000% return on your investment, and you do that just seven times, you would have more than the entire world money supply! In this light, the words of Jesus become even more intriguing:

> "Do not lay up for yourselves treasures upon earth, where moth and rust destroy, and where thieves break in and steal. But lay up for yourselves treasures in heaven, where neither moth nor rust destroys, and where thieves do not break in or steal" (Mat. 6:19-20).

How do you lay up treasure in heaven? The Great Commission in Mat. 28:19 says, to "Go into all the world and make disciples." And in Mat. 4:19, Jesus said: "Follow Me, and I will make you fishers of men." With that understanding, let's examine the verse this book is based on, Proverbs 29:25:

> "The fear of man brings a snare, but he who trusts in the Lord will be exalted."

The word translated "snare" in our English Bible comes from a Hebrew word that is used both literally and figuratively for a noose. The word picture is that of a hunter who sets a noose for an animal. Once the victim is caught, it is either held in captivity or eaten. 1 Peter 5:8 says:

> "Be of sober spirit, be on the alert. Your adversary, the devil, prowls about like a roaring lion, seeking someone to devour."

The hunter in this case is Satan, and *you* are the hunted one. His plan to keep the church quiet seems to be working. According to George Barna, only 2% of people who claim to be Christians regularly share their faith with unbelievers. Satan spreads the net, and the fear of man drives us right into it. Sometimes it's blatant; sometimes it's subtle. We smile when we should frown, we laugh when we should remain silent or, worse, we remain silent when we should speak. To remain silent when we should speak is to compromise with the world, the flesh, and the devil.

"Our Number-One Problem Is A Faulty Concept Of God."[2]

A right concept of God is the first step to living a full and satisfying life. You cannot know who you are until you know who God is. When you know who you are in relation to who He is, then you can begin to think and live in light of eternity.

There is some consolation in knowing this. None of us are immune from this spiritual disease known as the fear of man. Even the great cloud of witnesses who have gone on before us experienced it. But, as they grew in wisdom and experience, and after being baptized in the Holy Spirit, they learned to overcome the fear of man in the strength of the Lord.

Abraham, the "father of our faith," was willing to give up his wife to another man, not once but twice, because of the fear of man. His son, Isaac, did the same thing with his wife, Rebecca. Even the disciples, who were eyewitnesses of the miracles of Christ, fled when the heat was on. The Apostle Peter denied even knowing Jesus not once, not twice, but three times! And, three times in Matthew chapter 10 Jesus said: "Do not fear man." Note His dire warning in verse 28:

> "And do not fear those who kill the body, but are unable to kill the soul; but rather fear Him who is able to destroy both soul and body in hell."

If someone puts a gun to my head and says, "Renounce Christ, or die," I would have to say, "You mean you're threatening me with heaven?" For the Christian, death is not the end, it's the glorious beginning. You haven't found anything worth living for until you've found something worth dying for!

In Isaiah 57:11, God the Father said:

> "Whom have you so dreaded and feared that you have been false to Me, and have neither remembered Me, nor pondered this in your hearts? Is it not because I have long been silent that you do not fear Me?"

May I Be Excused, Please?

In the Old Testament, you were excused from war for any of three reasons: (1) If you had just married a wife, (2) If you had planted a vineyard and had not tasted the fruit of the vine, or (3) If you were afraid.

Why would being afraid excuse you? Because the morale of one man had the potential of destroying the morale of the entire army.[3]

When God commissioned Gideon to go to battle, He said (in effect), "Gideon, I want you to go to battle, and I guarantee your victory. The only thing is, you have too many men. If you win with this many men, you may be tempted to touch the glory that belongs to Me. I want you to tell everybody who's afraid to go home." He had 32,000 men, and 22,000 of them admitted they were wimps and went home.

The Fear Of Man Is Idolatry

Idolatry is rival worship. Placing any created thing before the Creator is spiritual adultery—an abomination to God. In James 4:4 this indictment was handed down by God Himself:

> "You adulteresses, do you not know that friendship with the world is hostility toward God? Therefore whoever wishes to be a friend of the world makes himself an enemy of God."

God couldn't be clearer when in Isaiah 51:12 He says:

> "I, even I, am He who comforts you. Who are you that you are afraid of man who will die, and of the son of man who is made like grass?"

I don't mean to brag, but I'm not afraid of grass at all. In fact, I cut the grass at home. Honestly, I wouldn't be afraid if there were a whole bale of hay right behind me! God is saying, in essence, "Let's look at this in perspective. A man may live for seventy or eighty years, and then he dies like grass. It is absurd to be in dread of a dying man. I am the God who is, the God who was, and the God who always will be, without beginning and without end. I AM the eternal, self-existent One. Why are you afraid of a man who will die? A man can't save you, and a man can't condemn you. Only I can do that."

A Profound Real-Life Illustration

I was out of town sitting in a hotel watching the Discovery Channel when I saw a spectacular illustration of the fear of man. There was a teacher telling a sixth-grade class of students that they were going to do an experiment. The teacher said, "I'm going to hold up two cards. One with a long line and the other has a short line on it. We are going to bring in a student who is unaware of our experiment to see how he or she will react. When I hold up the cards I want you to purposely answer incorrectly. I'll show you both cards and ask, "How many of you think this is the shorter of the two lines when it is really the longer one. At that point, you all raise your hands. Okay?" Everyone agreed. Then the extra student was brought in. The teacher held up the two cards. With the long line in her right hand and the short line in her left hand, she waved the long line and asked, "How many of you think this is the shorter of the two lines; raise your hands?" Everybody raised their hands. The child who was unaware of what was going on also raised his hand. They tried it again and again and each time the children raised their hands—knowing in their hearts they were answering incorrectly.

When I got home, I related this story to my wife and children. I said to my kids, "I would like to think if one of you were in that classroom, knowing everyone was answering incorrectly, you would have stood up and asked, 'Does anybody have a ruler?'" This represents another classic example of the fear of man. These young people were willing to throw their common sense and dignity right out the window rather than appear to be different from the crowd. It's called *peer pressure*. Just remember, it's better to be what you is than what you ain't because, if you is what you ain't, then you ain't what you is.

In Church, Too?

Sometimes when I am in church on Sunday morning I become overwhelmed when the worship is being offered up. I think of where the Lord has taken me from, how good He has been to me, and the fact that I don't deserve it. Sometimes I just close my eyes and lift my hands (which is the universal gesture of surrender, and the universal gesture of victory). There are people who mistakenly associate this practice with a particular sect of Christianity. Not so. It was ordained by the Apostle Paul himself, in a letter to his young protégé, Timothy. In 1 Tim. 2:8, Paul writes:

"I want men everywhere to lift up holy hands unto the Lord."

After church one day, a lady came up to me and said, "I wish I had the courage to raise my hands in church." This dear lady wanted to, in child-like faith, lift her hands to worship the God who gave her life, but was paralyzed by the fear of man.

Beware Of The Leaven Of The Pharisees

Pride and jealousy among the clergy in America are epidemic. This is not a new phenomenon. Remember what happened to King Saul after David killed Goliath? Upon returning to Jerusalem after the battle, the women of the city came out to greet the victors. In celebration the women were singing, "Saul has slain his thousands, but David has slain his ten thousands!" Saul went berserk with jealousy and tried to kill his best warrior. It was this same spirit that motivated the Pharisees to *murder* Jesus!

Because of insecurity (which is usually based on pride), many in leadership are jealous and fearful of others who also may be qualified to lead. All of us have our own stories of how the fear of man is played out every day. But when we talk about putting *man* before God, our eternal destiny is on the line. Remember, the fear of man is idolatry.

Fortunately, there are exceptions to this rule, but generally speaking, the church has become so politically correct, pastors are afraid of offending anyone. Many of our church members have the telephone-company mentality. If I don't like it here, I can get a better deal at the church down the street.

For the same reason church discipline (for the most part) has gone the way of high-button shoes—it's a thing of the past. The reason? Pastors and elders are afraid of losing members. The rationale goes something like this: If I offend people, they might leave and go to another church. If enough people leave, I'll be out of a job.

Much of our preaching is weak for the same reason. Many churches are merely social clubs with an emphasis on spirituality. For them, it's okay to have church on Sunday, as long as it doesn't interfere with lunch or the game.

The Real Reason People Reject Christianity

The name of Jesus can clear out a room faster than any other name in the world. Mention the name of any other so-called religious leader, and nobody cares. Why does the name Jesus have so much power? All He did was say things like, "Love your enemies. If your enemy is hungry, feed, him. If he's thirsty, give him a drink. If he takes your shirt, give him your coat, too!"

Well, Jesus also said, "I am the light of the world." The reason men hate Jesus is because the light exposes the darkness and men love darkness rather than the light. Light and darkness are metaphors for good and evil.

People reject Christianity not because they can't believe; it's because they won't. It's a matter of the will, not the intellect. They know that becoming a follower of Jesus Christ would require a radical change in their lifestyle. In John 7:17, Jesus said:

> "If any man is willing to do His will, he shall know of the teaching, whether it is of God, or whether I speak from Myself."

Many people make up wild excuses in their minds. Some believe if they became Christians, God would immediately ship them off to Africa as missionaries! But in most cases, the real issue is not, "is Christianity true," but "what would my 'friends' think if I became a Jesus freak or a religious fanatic?" That's the fear of man vs. the fear of God in a nutshell. Jesus put it in perspective better than anyone before or since:

> "For what is a man profited, if he shall gain the whole world, and lose his own soul? Or what shall a man give in exchange for his soul?"

The Fear Of Man On A Larger Scale

Chicken Little was a little chicken who made the big time with a prophecy of doom and gloom. Her mantra was straight and to the point: "The sky is falling!" Well, with the possibilities of nuclear Armageddon and World War III, and the realities of terrorism, the Middle East War, corruption in government and business, the collapse of the US economy, earthquakes, famine, floods, droughts, fuel shortages, pandemics and emerging diseases, violence in the streets, immorality, organized crime, broken families, unsaved loved ones, unemployment, apostasy in the church, Christianity becoming criminalized, and much more, I understand why "we the people" are very concerned about the future. Humanly speaking, we have great reason to be troubled. But, spiritually speaking, we have even greater reason *not* to be. In John 14:1-3, Jesus Christ said:

> "Let not your heart be troubled; believe in God, believe also in Me. In My Father's house are many mansions; if it were not so, I would have told you; for I go to prepare a place for you. And if I go and prepare a place for you, I will come again, and receive you to Myself, that where I am, there you may be also."

Understanding this verse in its historical context gives us the power we need to experience the peace it promises. The disciples of Jesus were sure that He was the answer to all of their problems. He could give sight to the blind, feed thousands with just a couple loaves of bread and a few fish, and even raise the dead! In this light, they were sure that not only was Jesus going to overthrow the Roman Empire, but they were going to rule the world with Him. The disciples were already arguing with each other over who was going to sit on His right hand and on His left in the kingdom.

Suddenly, the dream began to turn into a nightmare. Jesus began to tell them things that were deeply troubling. Incredibly, He began to speak to them of His own death! Then, point-blank, He said, "One of you will betray Me." Each man must have been haunted by the distinct possibility that he was the traitor. Then Jesus told them, "I am leaving, and where I am going, you cannot come." Then, Jesus looked at Peter, their leader, and said, "Before the cock crows, you will deny Me three times." That is the background for Jesus' statement in John 14:1-3. Here is the redemption factor:

> While the disciples had great reason to be troubled, they had even greater reason not to be. The same holds true for you and me!

In John 16:33, Jesus said:

> "These things I have spoken to you, that in Me you may have peace. In the world you have tribulation, but take courage; I have overcome the world."

Keep reading!

Small Group Questions

1. Imagine this: You go out to a restaurant with your spouse. The hostess comes up and asks, "Table for two?" Your spouse replies, "We would like separate tables, please." You ask, "Why would we do that?" Your spouse says: "Well, I wouldn't want anybody to know we were married." How would that make you feel? How do you think it makes Jesus feel when we are embarrassed or ashamed to be seen with Him in public (by carrying a Bible, praying in a restaurant, going to church, etc.)?

2. What do we learn from the children who purposely answered incorrectly to the long-line / short-line question?

3. What do you think Jesus means in John 8:24?

4. What comes to your mind when you think about God?

5. What are the implications of having a faulty concept of God?

6. Jesus sent His disciples out in twos. What are some of the reasons you think He did that?

7. Read Jas. 4:4. What is idolatry? Why is it an abomination?

8. Many people are psychologically oriented rather than truth–oriented. What does that mean and what are its implications?

9. Was there anything in this chapter that spoke to your heart, and if so, what was it, and why?

10. What is the main reason people reject Christianity? How does knowing that help you be a better witness?

CHAPTER TWO

The Greatest Demonstration Of Power Anyone Has Ever Seen
The Fear Of God

In northwestern Saudi Arabia, out in the middle of the desert and surrounded by oceans of sand, there is a small "top secret" military outpost. A handful of Saudi marksmen armed with automatic weapons and guard dogs patrol an area surrounded by a chain-link fence. Their mission? To keep any and all curiosity seekers away from this site. In addition to the military patrol (remember this is in the middle of nowhere), there is a large sign posted in front of the guard house, outside the fence, carrying this warning in Arabic and in English:

> "This is a protected archeological site. All trespassers will be prosecuted."

So, what's behind the fence that the Saudi government does not want the world to see? Shrouded in secrecy is an 8,465 foot mountain known to the local Bedouins as Jabal Musa. You can find it on a good map under the name Jabal Al Lawz.

So, why would anyone want to "protect" a mountain out in the middle of the desert? If the truth were known, and if the Saudis allowed biblical scholars, archeologists, and journalists to examine this site, it would be hailed as one of the greatest archeological discoveries of all time! The effect, however, would be a disaster for the Saudis. What happened here is so significant, and the evidence is so overwhelmingly conclusive, if word got out, many people would be willing to risk their lives by sneaking into the country just to see it. Some already have, and *that* is why the area is guarded. Since the Saudis preferred method of dealing with "infidels" is beheading, the potential to create *another* international crisis, similar to the fight for sovereignty over the Temple Mount in Jerusalem, is far too great.

What Is So Unusual About This Mountain?

At the base of the mountain there is a huge formation of boulders (some weighing hundreds of tons) carefully placed on top of one another three stories high, 100 feet across, and flat on top. This engineering feat required a large number of people who were *highly motivated,* and had a good deal of experience moving stones of this magnitude. Whoever it was that went to all this trouble also had a fetish for cattle. Etched into the sides of this giant memorial are pictures of cows and bulls. Strange indeed, since cattle are not indigenous to the desert. In addition, there are large piles of smaller rocks every 400 yards forming a semicircle around the mountain. They appear to serve as boundary markers, as if to say, "This far, and no farther." At the foot of the mountain there is a V-shaped pit with carefully placed stones along the sides to form walls. It is believed that this area was used for animal sacrifice. Next to that there are 12 hand-hewn pillars made of stone, which represent a memorial of something very significant to someone. The question is, to whom?

Most unusual of all is the fact that the mountain itself (made of solid granite rock) is brown, but the peak (the top third of the mountain) is shiny black. It appears as if the top of the mountain had been exposed to an intense heat and melted by a giant incinerator!

Scholars and archeologists who have examined the sum of evidence on and around this mountain (based on eye-witness accounts, pictures, and video tape smuggled out of the country), are convinced that this is the actual site where God gave Moses the Ten Commandments! All of the evidence matches perfectly with the biblical account of the Israelites Exodus from Egypt. The traditional site, on the Sinai Peninsula, matches none of the facts recorded in the Bible.

Providentially, it only rains a fraction of an inch every ten years in this area, so all the effects left by God and 2-3 million Israelites have been perfectly preserved for thousands of years. There are a number of great books and videos documenting the facts of this discovery that are nothing short of spectacular![1]

So What Does All This Have To Do With The Fear Of Man Vs. The Fear Of God?

God's message from Mt. Sinai was accompanied by a display of sight and sound so terrifying, when it was over, the people begged Moses never to let God speak to them directly again. They were convinced that one more manifestation like that would literally kill them (Ex. 20:19). This raises a most important and fundamental question. Why would God do such a thing to His own people? What was the point in almost scaring them to death? The answer is found at the end of the story:

> "And all the people perceived the thunder and the lightning flashes and the sound of the trumpet and the mountain smoking; and when the people saw it, they trembled and stood at a distance."

When it was over, they said to Moses:

> "'Speak to us yourself and we will listen; but let not God speak to us, lest we die.' And Moses said to the people, 'Do not be afraid; for God has come in order to test you, and in order that the fear of Him may remain with you, so that you may not sin'" (Ex. 20:20).

There is our answer; that we might fear the consequences of sinning against God. The benefits of understanding what sin is, and what its consequences are, cannot be overstated:

- The demonstration at Sinai was to show us how much God hates sin, and how we should fear its consequences.
- It is sin that separates us from God (Isa. 59:2).
- Sin is what Jesus came to save us from (Mat. 1:21).
- The wages of sin is death (Rom. 3:23).
- We sin when we transgress any of God's commandments.

God is perfectly holy and just. He dwells in unapproachable light. He cannot overlook even one sin or He would be unjust. Do you know what God wants to save you from on judgment day? The just penalty of sin which is separation from Him. His love for man is so great, He gave His only begotten Son to take the punishment for our sin upon Himself!

What Exactly Is The Fear Of The Lord?

The word translated "fear" from the Greek New Testament is the word *phobos*. That is where we get the word "phobia" from. It literally means:

1. Fear, dread, terror; what strikes terror.
2. Reverence (respect).

So, there is a negative fear, such as terror, and a positive fear, as in reverence and respect for authority. The fear of God entails both. This is where true wisdom begins.

Here Is What The Bible Actually Says About The Fear Of God

I have paraphrased the following verses. These are the attitudes, attributes, characteristics, qualities, and effects that define and accompany the "fear of God."

- Exod. 18:21: Men who fear God are men of truth; they hate dishonest gain.

- Job 28:28: The fear of the Lord is wisdom, which means to "depart from evil" that is "understanding."

- Ps. 33:8-9: We fear and revere the LORD, because He spoke the universes into existence.

- Ps. 111:10: Those who fear God are those who keep His commandments and have great understanding. They understand the implications of God's eternal nature.

- Prv. 8:13: Those who fear the LORD love the things that God loves and hate the things that God hates such as: evil, pride, arrogance, and the perverted mouth.

- Prv. 14:26: Those who fear the Lord have strong confidence.

- Prv. 15:33: Those who fear the LORD recognize that humility is a virtue, not a weakness.

- Prv. 23:17: Those who fear God do not envy wicked people.

- Eccl. 12:13: Those who fear the Lord keep His commandments because they understand the meaning of life.

- Mat. 10:28: Those who fear the Lord live in light of eternity. They have the fear of man in proper context.

- 2 Cor. 5:10-11: Those who fear the Lord are acutely aware that they are accountable to God when life is over.

- 2 Cor. 7:1: Those who fear the Lord have a passion for holiness and right living.

- 2 Pet. 3:10-12: Those who fear the Lord know that Judgment Day is coming on this world.

- Heb. 10:31: Those who fear God know that it is a terrifying thing for the unsaved to fall into the hands of the living God.

Let's Put It Into Perspective

Now, think of some of the things that have caused you to experience fear in the past. How about the sound of thunder? When it is close enough, it can be so loud it really scares you. That is how God got Martin Luther's attention. Have you ever experienced an earthquake or a man wielding a gun? How about when you see a policeman in your rear-view mirror, and your speedometer tells you you're over the limit? Does that scare you? Well, if these things put fear into our hearts, how much more should a thinking person have a positive fear and reverence for Someone who is so holy and pure He dwells in unapproachable light, and has the power to speak the universe into existence and it becomes reality?

I Fear No Man

Martin Luther King, Jr., by his own admission, had some serious moral failures. I do not condone immorality, but one thing I did admire about this man was his lion-hearted boldness. In the 1960's, King was warned that if he did not end his fight for civil rights in America, he would be assassinated. In one of the greatest speeches of his life he said, "I have a dream. I have a dream that someday little black boys and little white boys will be able to play together. I have a dream, and I have been to the mountain-top, and I fear no man, for mine eyes have seen the glory of the coming of the Lord!"[3] Not long after that he was shot and killed by an assassin's bullet. What I admire about him is the fact that he was willing to fight for a just cause, knowing it would probably cost him his life.

When I stand before God I hope to hear the words, "Well done, thou good and faithful servant. For you did not live for the praise of men, but for the praise that comes from the only God. You were faithful in a few things; enter into the joy of your Master!" I also hope I will be able to say something on that day as well. I hope I can look at the Lord and say, "I have finished the work You gave me to do."

Small Group Questions

1. What does it mean to "fear God?"

2. How is the fear of the Lord a positive thing?

3. Read Mat. 7:24-27. What is Jesus literally talking about?

4. Read Mat. 10:27-28. What is the point?

5. How does having a proper understanding of the nature of God help us to overcome the fear of man?

6. What was the point of God almost scaring His own people to death at Mt. Sinai?

7. Have each member of the group read one of these verses out loud in an attempt to answer the question, "What is the relevance of the Ten Commandments today?" Mat. 5:21, 27-28, Rom. 2:15; 3:20-21; 7:7; 8:7, Gal.3:24, 1 Tim. 1:8, 1 Jn.3:14, Rev.12:17.

8. Explain, paraphrase, illustrate, or prove John 16:33.

9. Read Mat. 25:31-46. Who or what does God want to save you from?

10. Why can the name of Jesus clear out a room faster than any other name in the world?

Grasshoppers And Giants, Warriors And Wimps

The Classic Example Of The Fear Of Man Vs. The Fear Of God
(and its consequences)

In order to understand why Israel has suffered more than any other nation in history (and what that has to do with you), you need to understand this sobering truth found in Luke 12:48:

> "From him to whom much is given, much will be required."

I naturally expect more from my older children than my younger ones because they are more knowledgeable, more experienced, and thus more capable. The law of reciprocity was established by God, and is just as real and immutable as the law of gravity or Newton's law of motion (for every action there is an equal and opposite reaction). Galatians 6:7 says:

> "Do not be deceived; God is not mocked; for whatever a man sows, this he will also reap. "

The same principle is applied to teachers in James 3:1:

> "Let not many of you become teachers, my brethren, knowing that as such we shall incur a stricter judgment."

The more God gives you the more He expects from you. If you are faithful in little things, God will entrust you with more (Luke 16:10-11). The opposite is also true. Reciprocity either works for you or against you. The choice is yours.

When you look at the ancient Israelites, you see a group of people who had the bar set higher than for any other race in human history. The Jews were called "God's chosen people," not because they were better or smarter than everybody else, but because they were *chosen* to do a job. Their mission was to reveal the hand of the invisible God and His plan of redemption to the world. This would be accomplished in three ways.

First, as a nation, Israel would serve as an object lesson to the rest of the world. God promised the Israelites: if they would love, trust, and obey Him, in His sovereign power, He would exalt them far above all the other nations. Spiritually, intellectually, economically, militarily, and politically they would stand alone as the greatest nation on earth.

If, on the other hand they rebelled, if they failed to do what they were called and equipped to do, if they loved the world more than the God who created the world, God would allow the curse of sin to run its course on the nation. Either way, the sovereign power and divine nature of the invisible God would be clearly seen through Israel; whether blessing or the curse, the choice was theirs (see Deut. 28 and Lev. 26).

Second, the prophets and the apostles were chosen by God to produce the sacred scriptures. Most of the Bible was written in Israel by Israelites (Luke was the only Gentile writer). The prophets foretold Israel's future in spectacular detail. Today, thousands of years after the Bible was written, the facts of Israel's history and it's present situation are undeniable.

Third, God would reveal Himself and His plan of redemption through the incarnation—Jesus Christ Himself. Jesus came to earth as a Jew, He shed His blood on Israelite soil, and He offered His life as a sacrifice for sin. This occurred on the exact spot Abraham offered Isaac thousands of years earlier on Mt. Moriah. This is what John 4:29b means when it says:

"...salvation is from the Jews."

Setting The Stage

The Jewish nation began some 4000 years ago with one man—Abraham. Abraham had Isaac and Isaac had Jacob. Jacob had twelve sons who became the twelve tribes of the nation of Israel. The next scene introduces Joseph, who saves the family from starvation in Egypt.

After 400 years in Egypt, the original family of 70 became a nation of 2-3 million people. Moses brings them out of Egypt to Mt. Sinai where God gives them their Constitution and their Declaration of Independence—the Ten Commandments.

The promise to Abraham, beginning in Genesis 12, was that one of his descendants would be a blessing to the whole world. Now we *know* that the blessing God promised Abraham was nothing less than the redemption of mankind and the universe itself from the curse of sin.

In the Exodus from Egypt, God demonstrated His faithfulness to the Hebrew people again and again. Miracle after miracle proved that absolutely nothing was impossible with God. He wanted them to love and trust Him no matter what would come their way. God was preparing them to enter the Promised Land, where He would fulfill His glorious plan of redeeming the world.

First, He delivered them from Egyptian slavery with ten mighty plagues, one at a time. Each was more devastating than those preceding it, and each carried a message. They were uniquely designed to show the Hebrews (and the Egyptians) that the so-called gods of Egypt were no gods at all. He was the one true almighty, all-powerful, all-knowing, eternal God, and there is no other God besides Him.

At that time, the Egyptian empire was the greatest military power on earth. God demonstrated that they were utterly powerless against Him. There was nothing, not even their demonic magic arts, that could thwart the plan of God.

God saved His people again, when the Egyptians came after them in the wilderness, with a cloud of darkness. Then He parted the Red Sea so the Hebrews could escape on dry ground. What a sight that must have been! When the Egyptians tried to follow after the Israelites, God closed the sea and the enemies of God were drowned. Water from rocks, and bread from heaven—God provided for their every need. The culmination of God's demonstration of power came at Mt. Sinai when He came down out of heaven and audibly gave them the Ten Commandments.

With That As A Foundation, Here Is The lesson God Has For Us

Remember, this is recorded for our instruction, so read it carefully. Here is an abbreviated version of what happened to the Israelites on their way to the "land of promise."

In Deut. 1:22, where we discover that the idea to spy out the land actually originated with the people, not God. So, rather than taking God at His word and following Him in the battle, they wanted to assess the situation themselves. They would spy out the land to develop their own military strategy.

The whole point in bringing them out of Egypt was to bring them into the land that God swore by Himself to give them! In God's economy, Israel's victory over the Canaanites would serve a dual purpose. The Canaanites were exceedingly wicked and had been so for hundreds of years (see Genesis 15). A decisive military victory would serve as God's hand of judgment against them. Second, it would provide the real estate His people needed to establish their nation.

So, the twelve spies went in to assess what the land was like, whether the people were strong or weak, what their numbers were, how the cities were built, what the terrain was like, and to bring back some fruit. They cut down a single cluster of grapes that was so enormous, they had to carry it on a pole between two men.

The irony of this is, none of these details mattered. God had already guaranteed their victory. This was all His idea in the first place. This was the Holy Land where God would redeem the world with His own blood (Acts 20:28). Here is what Moses told them in Deut. 1:30:

> "The LORD your God who goes before you will Himself fight on your behalf, just as He did for you in Egypt before your eyes."

When the spies returned, they showed Moses and all the people of Israel the fruit and provided this report:

> "We went in to the land; and it certainly does flow with milk and honey, and this is its fruit. Nevertheless, the people who live in the land are strong, and the cities are fortified and very large."

That little *nevertheless* means they were not walking by faith, but by sight, and Caleb knew it. Discerning the situation, he quickly jumped in and said:

> "We should by all means go up and take possession of it, for we shall surely overcome it."

Unfortunately, ten of the men who had gone up with him said, "We are not able to go up against the people, for they are too strong for us. The land devours its inhabitants; and all the men are of great size." Then they added this:

> "We became like grasshoppers in our own sight, and so we were in their sight."

One of the most amazing things about this report is the fact that God isn't even mentioned! Rather than turning to God for help, this report "melted their hearts." All that night the people "grumbled and complained." They accused God of hating them and wanting to destroy them and their children. The consensus was they would have been better off had they died in the wilderness (ironically, they did die in the wilderness but their children entered the Promised Land). Then, they wanted to appoint a leader and *return to Egypt!*

What were these people thinking? Can you imagine what kind of welcome *they* would have received in Egypt? The last time they were in town, the entire nation was totally devastated by ten plagues. All the firstborn of the Egyptians were killed, and the entire army was drowned in the Red Sea! The Egyptians were so happy to see them leave, they gave them articles of silver, gold, and clothing on their way out. It was Egypt's way of saying, "Don't call us; we'll call you." Thus the Hebrews "plundered the Egyptians." What they were proposing, in light of all that God had done for them, is mind-boggling.

At this point, Moses, Aaron, Joshua, and Caleb fell on their faces in deep distress. They tore their clothes, and they pleaded with the people:

> "'Do not rebel against the LORD; and do not fear the people of the land, for they shall be our prey. Their protection has been removed from them, and the LORD is with us; do not fear them.

The Israelites wanted to stone their own leaders, abandon God's plan, and go back to slavery in Egypt! That is when the Lord stepped in:

> "How long will this people spurn Me? And how long will they not believe in Me, despite all the signs which I have performed in their midst?"

> "So the LORD said…'Surely all the men who have seen My glory and My signs, which I performed in Egypt and in the wilderness, yet have put Me to the test these ten times and have not listened to My voice, shall by no means see the land which I swore to their fathers, nor shall any of those who spurned Me see it. But My servant Caleb, because he has had a different spirit and has followed Me fully, I will bring into the land which he entered, and his descendants shall take possession of it.'"

A Classic Example Of
The Fear Of Man Vs. The Fear Of God
And Its Consequences

It is a great insult to the power, the honor, and the glory of God when people fear the creature more than the Creator. Not to believe God's Word is to call Him a liar. God called their unbelief *rebellion*!

Even in this life, if a soldier refuses to obey a direct order from a commanding officer in a time of war, this is mutiny, a crime that is punishable by death! In this light, Rev. 21:8 is sobering, to say the least:

> "But for the cowardly and unbelieving and abominable and murderers and immoral persons and sorcerers and idolaters and all liars, their part will be in the lake that burns with fire and brimstone, which is the second death."

We know from Numbers 11:1 that God hates complaining. All complaining is rebellion against the sovereignty of God. Imagine what it would be like to take a neighbor on vacation with you and your family. You are all looking forward to a great escape, and you're picking up the tab, but your neighbor complains about everything: "It's too hot; it's too cold; I don't like this; I don't like that; I'm sorry I came on this trip; I want to go home!" It does not take long for this kind of attitude to take its toll on even the most patient and gracious person.

Remember the principle found in Luke 12:48, "From him to whom much is given much will be required." While it is true that the ancient Hebrews had the advantage of seeing God's miracles, we not only have the record of those miracles, but we also have the complete plan of redemption as revealed in the New Testament. The Old Testament prophets themselves did not fully understand how God's plan of redemption would be completed. The prophets (and the angels who are watching all this unfold in real time) longed to look into the things we take for granted, namely, that Jesus Christ was the Lamb of God. His sacrifice was sufficient to pay for all of mankind's sin once and for all. No more animal sacrifices would be needed. The promise to Abraham, that all the families of the earth would be blessed through one of his descendants, was fulfilled in Jesus Christ.

While the blessings and curses recorded in Deut. 28 and Lev. 26 were originally and uniquely intended for Israel, the New Testament says that the things that happened to the Israelites were written for our instruction and for our example. The word translated "example" is *tupos* in Greek. It's a type. In a doctrinal sense, it's the prefiguring of a person or event. It's a pattern with a warning.

> "Now these things happened as examples for us, that we should not crave evil things, as they also craved. And do not be idolaters, as some of them were; as it is written, 'The people sat down to eat and drink, and stood up to play.'
>
> "Nor let us act immorally, as some of them did, and twenty-three thousand fell in one day. Nor let us try the Lord, as some of them did, and were destroyed by the serpents. Nor grumble, as some of them did, and were destroyed by the destroyer.
>
> "Now these things happened to them as an example, and they were written for our instruction, upon whom the ends of the ages have come" 1 Cor. 10:6-11.

The Recognition Of A Problem Is Half Of The Solution

The reason so many Christians, spiritually speaking, are not resting in the "Promised Land flowing with milk and honey" is clear. We are guilty of doing exactly the same thing the ancient Israelites did. God called them to go and possess the land, but the children of light were intimidated by the children of darkness. They assessed the situation themselves and decided it was too difficult. Leaving God completely out of the equation, they were defeated by their own sin—unbelief.

Like the Israelites of old, the church has also been chosen for a mission. It's called "The Great Commission." In Matthew 28:19, Jesus said:

> "Go into all the world and make disciples of all nations."

While it is true that we are not all called to preach, according to this verse, we are *all* called to reach. We are rebelling against the command of God if we are not involved in evangelism and making disciples.

The enemy has come in like a flood, and most of the "good men" simply do nothing. For a season Satan is prevailing and God is going to allow sin to run its course. The saying, "If we don't learn anything from history, we are destined to repeat it," is absolutely true. That is exactly what the Bible is saying in 1 Cor. 10:6. There is no way to escape this principle. God is not unjust. He warned us thousands of years in advance. All of us will stand before Almighty God when life is over and be judged. We will all give an account to Him of what we did with what we had. Contrary to popular opinion, that includes all true believers. The following verses were written to the church:

> "Now if any man builds upon the foundation with gold, silver, precious stones, wood, hay, straw, each man's work will become evident; for the day will show it, because it is to be revealed with fire; and the fire itself will test the quality of each man's work. If any man's work which he has built upon it remains, he shall receive a reward. If any man's work is burned up, he shall suffer loss; but he himself shall be saved, yet so as through fire" 1 Cor. 3:12.

> "For we must all appear before the judgment seat of Christ, that each one may be recompensed for his deeds in the body, according to what he has done, whether good or bad" 2 Cor. 5:10.

"For it is time for judgment to begin with the household of God; and if it begins with us first, what will be the outcome for those who do not obey the gospel of God?" 1 Pet. 4:17.

Grandma's Duck

Steve Farrar, in his excellent book, *Finishing Strong*, tells a story that goes something like this. A boy and his sister went to visit their grandparents in the country. Grandpa gave his grandson Billy a slingshot. In the woods Billy tried, but missed everything he shot at. On his way home he spotted grandma's pet duck in the backyard. He picked up a rock, fired at the duck, and bulls-eye, right in the head. Grandma's duck was dead. Looking both ways, he grabbed the duck, ran into the barn, and hid it under some hay. He walked back in the house just in time to hear grandma call for sister Sally to help with dinner. Sally called back and said, "Billy's going to help with dinner tonight, Grandma!" Billy looks at Sally, and Sally whispers, "I saw what you did to Grandma's duck!" After dinner, Grandma asks Sally, "Would you please help clear the table dear?" And Sally replies, "Billy's going to clear the table tonight Grandma." Billy looks at her, and without speaking, she moves her lips and says, "Remember the duck!" So, Billy clears the table. Well, the same thing happened with the dinner dishes too. Finally, Grandma looks at Billy and says, "Okay, Billy, what's up between you and Sally?" So, with tears in his eyes, Billy tells his grandmother what happened to her pet duck. The grandmother says to her grandson, "It's okay, Billy; I was looking out the window and I saw the whole thing. I knew you didn't mean to kill my duck. I was just wondering how long you would let your sister make a slave out of you."

How long will you allow the fear of man to make a slave out of you? As long as you are afraid to get real with God, you'll never know the freedom, the joy, and the rest He has prepared for those who love Him. Here is something you may have never considered before. To love the God who created you is the most normal, natural, sane, rational, intelligent thing a human being can do. If someone were to say to me, "You mean you're one of those 'Jesus freaks'"? I would say, "You mean you're not?" Remember, when you're right about God and you're right with God, the children of light need never be intimidated by the children of darkness.

Small Group Questions

1. In light of I Cor. 10:6-11, what are the parallels between the Israelites' failure to take the Promised Land and the Christians' reluctance to share the Gospel?

2. Read Luke 12:48. What do you think it means? What does it tell us about God? What effect should this have on us?

3. Who do you think God would consider cowards, and how does He feel about them? Check Rev. 21:8.

4. What does the church know that the prophets did not fully understand? What then is our responsibility before God?

5. Read 2 Cor. 5:1-7. What does it mean to walk by faith and not by sight? How should this impact your daily life?

6. Read Matthew 25:31-46. According to this verse, what is the fruit of those who are saved?

7. Should the church be held to a higher standard than the rest of the world? Why? Consider 2 Cor. 6:3.

8. Read 1 Cor. 3:12-15, 2 Cor. 5:10, and 1 Pet. 4:17. What do these verses tell us? How does that line up with what you have believed?

9. What was the difference between Joshua and Caleb and the other ten spies? What was the result of those differences?

10. In Gal. 5:22-23 we learn that "the fruit of the Spirit is...self control." What does this tell us about overcoming rebellion?

CHAPTER FOUR

What Does A 3,000-Year-Old Uncircumcised Philistine Have To Do With Me Anyway?

Fresh Insights From David And Goliath

The story of David and Goliath is another classic example of the fear of man vs. the fear of God. It is found in 1 Samuel chapter 17 of the Bible. The lessons are every bit as applicable to you and me today as they were 3,000 years ago. Before we go back to ancient Israel, I would like to add some salt to our story. It is found in Romans 15:4. This is what the New Testament says about the Old Testament:

> "For everything that was written in the past was written to teach us, so that through endurance and the encouragement of the Scriptures we might have hope."

In other words, there are timeless principles found in the Old Testament that God expects us to learn and grow from. The word *hope* in this verse is not used in the same way we might say, "I hope we're having spaghetti for dinner tonight." This word refers to the confident expectation, indeed an unshakable conviction, that God's promises are true. He is not a man that He should lie. I would doubt my heart and my eyes before I doubt Him.

In 1 Samuel 17:1 the Word of God says: "Now the Philistines gathered their armies for battle…." In verse 2 we find King Saul and the men of Israel gathered together in preparation for battle. In verse 3 we find the Philistines and the Israelites positioned on hilltops facing each other, with a valley between them. In verse 4, Goliath, the Philistine champion, comes forward. His height was "six cubits and a span." He was nine feet nine inches tall! Now notice verse 8:

"And he stood and shouted to the ranks of Israel, and said to them, 'Why do you come out to draw up in battle array? Am I not the Philistine and you servants of Saul? Choose a man for yourselves and let him come down to me. If he is able to fight with me and kill me, then we will become your servants; but if I prevail against him and kill him, then you shall become our servants and serve us.'"

In verse 10 Goliath said:

"'I defy the ranks of Israel this day; give me a man that we may fight together.' When Saul and all Israel heard these words of the Philistine, they were dismayed and greatly afraid."

Folks, "greatly afraid" means the Israelites were paralyzed with fear. Saul has been anointed by the Prophet Samuel as Israel's first king. Unfortunately, Saul only has a half-hearted commitment to the God, king, and country thing. At this point, his lack of leadership was crippling the Israeli army.

Now, getting back to battle, in 1 Sam 17:16 we read:

"And the Philistine came forward morning and evening for forty days, and took his stand."

Every morning and every evening this giant would challenge the Israelites to send out a man to do battle with him. One man from each side would represent the people of that nation. If the Philistines won, the Hebrews would become their slaves. If the Hebrews won, the Philistines would serve them.

Meanwhile, back at the ranch, our hero, David, oblivious to what was happening on the battle front, is tending the family sheep! This was the lowest and most humble job you could have. Three of David's older brothers are with King Saul on the front-lines of the "battle." David's father, Jesse, now commissions David to bring some provisions to his brothers and to check on their welfare. Take at look at what happens when David comes on the scene in verse 20:

"So David arose early in the morning and left the flock with a keeper and took the supplies and went as Jesse had commanded him. And he came to the circle of the camp while the army was going out in battle array shouting the war cry.

And Israel and the Philistines drew up in battle array, army against army. Then David left his baggage in the care of the baggage keeper and ran to the battle line and entered in order to greet his brothers. As he was talking with them, behold, the champion, the Philistine from Gath named Goliath, was coming up from the army of the Philistines, and he spoke these same words; and David heard them. When all the men of Israel saw the man, they fled from him and were greatly afraid. And the men of Israel said, 'Have you seen this man who is coming up? Surely he is coming up to defy Israel. And it will be that the king will enrich the man who kills him with great riches and will give him his daughter and make his father's house free in Israel.'"

King Saul, whom the Bible says is head and shoulders above everyone else in Israel, is too proud to admit that he is afraid. So, Saul is promising rewards to the man who kills Goliath. "You can live in Israel tax-free. I'll even throw in my daughter!" No takers. This had been going on for 40 days, every morning and every night! I suspect that most of the men were thinking something along these lines, "Gee, Saul, why don't *you* go fight Goliath? You're the biggest guy on the team and you're supposed to be our leader."

Then, David comes on the scene, and hears the blasphemy of the Philistine giant. The key that unlocks the treasure to this story is found in David's question in verse 26:

"For who is this uncircumcised Philistine, that he should taunt the armies of the living God?"

When David referred to Goliath as an *uncircumcised Philistine*, he understood something that the rest of his Hebrew brothers had either forgotten or simply did not believe. What was the significance of circumcision to the ancient Hebrews? Was it something men did for fun on a Saturday night like going out to get a tattoo after drinking too much? Hardly! The answer goes all the way back to Genesis chapter 17:9-10:

"God said further to Abraham, 'Now as for you, you shall keep My covenant, you and your descendants after you throughout their generations. This is My covenant, which you shall keep, between Me and you and your descendants after you: every male among you shall be circumcised.'"

David is saying in no uncertain terms, "Guys, have you forgotten who we are? We're the covenant people of God! Don't you remember Exodus 23:22 where God said, '...I will be an enemy to your enemies and will oppose those who oppose you?' And, what about Deut. 3:22? God said, 'Do not fear them, for the LORD your God is the one fighting for you.' And, what about Deut. 20:1? 'When you go out to battle against your enemies and see horses and chariots and people more numerous than you, do not be afraid of them; for the LORD your God, who brought you up from the land of Egypt, is with you.' We're the armies of the Living God! We come in the name of the LORD of hosts. This guy's not a part of the covenant!" What are you so afraid of?

David understands that he is in a covenant relationship with Almighty God, and ultimately, the battle and its outcome belong to Him! Now look at vs. 28:

> "Now Eliab his oldest brother heard when he spoke to the men; and Eliab's anger burned against David and he said, 'Why have you come down? And with whom have you left those few sheep in the wilderness? I know your insolence and the wickedness of your heart; for you have come down in order to see the battle.'"

Eliab, David's oldest brother, scorned David. This was the first battle David won before moving onto the next one. How many times and in how many ways have Christians been scorned by the world without justification? Look at David's response in verse 29:

> "But David said, 'What have I done now? Was it not just a question?'"

The word *now* implies that this was not the first time Eliab had scorned his little brother unjustly. David's response is reflective of a Spirit-filled man of God. Proverbs tells us that a soft answer turns away wrath. The Word also tells us that:

> "God resists the proud but gives grace to the humble."

David provides us with a stellar example of how a man of God responds under pressure. He could have shot back with something like, "Hey, big brother, you've been here for over a month. I don't see you stepping up to the plate to fight this dude." This would have been a perfect opportunity to brag about how he had killed lions and bears, but he makes no mention of it to his brother. Satan would have loved nothing more than to have God's people start fighting among themselves rather than focusing on the real enemy. David would have none of that. He knew this battle belonged to the LORD, and he was on God's side! For David, taking out Goliath would be no more difficult than breaking up a Girl Scout camp meeting. Knowing all this, he held his tongue and refused to shame or embarrass his brother. David exercised great humility and self-control. Not returning evil for evil, he controlled his temper and his pride.

The second battle is seen clearly in the exchange between David and King Saul in verses 31-37. When Saul heard that David was willing to fight the giant, he sent for him immediately. David assured the king that everyone could relax; Goliath was no problem. Saul responded by saying in effect, "I appreciate your heart, little brother, but this giant is out of your league. Goliath is a seasoned warrior, and you're just a kid." David, undaunted, undismayed, and unafraid, makes this gentle appeal:

> "While tending my father's sheep, I have killed both the lion and the bear. This uncircumcised Philistine will be just like one of them. The LORD who delivered me from the lion and the bear, He will deliver me from the hand of this Philistine."

Here again, we see David's humility and his dependence on God. He gives all the glory to the Lord for his victories over the wild beasts. Then King Saul (who bought his clothes at a big and tall men's store) puts his XXXL size armor on David, who wears a size small. Can't you just picture this? David is now wearing a suit of armor that is so big, he can't even walk in it. Realizing that Saul's armor would be more of a hindrance than a help, David takes it off and goes back to his street clothes! What does Saul's armor represent? The best the world has to offer without God—and it won't work. Then, Saul said to David, "Go, and may the LORD be with you." What a wimp!

David was not dependent upon worldly wise men, man-made suits of armor, or worldly strategies; David put on the full armor of God. He had truth for a belt, righteousness as a breastplate, his feet were prepared with good news that the victory was already won, he had faith for a shield, salvation as a helmet, and the sword of the Spirit which is the Word of God in his heart!

Bold as a lion, David walks down the hill into the valley to face the Philistine monster. Both armies are watching intensely. The Israelites cannot believe their eyes. Eliab's little brother, an untrained youth with no armor, no spear, and no experience, is going to fight the undisputed heavyweight champion of the Philistine army! I think it's safe to say that in their minds they believed Goliath was going to slaughter poor, defenseless, little David. *Amazingly, no one tried to stop him.* The Philistines must have been laughing hysterically at this obvious mismatch. Little did they know, this fight to the death would be a crushing defeat for the Philistines and the last day of Goliath's life. Now, here's the bell for Round One:

> "And he took his stick in his hand and chose for himself five smooth stones from the brook, and put them in the shepherd's bag which he had, even in his pouch, and his sling was in his hand; and he approached the Philistine. Then the Philistine came on and approached David, with the shield-bearer in front of him. When the Philistine looked and saw David, he disdained him; for he was but a youth, and ruddy, with a handsome appearance. And the Philistine said to David, 'Am I a dog, that you come to me with sticks?' And the Philistine cursed David by his gods."

The text says the Philistine "cursed" David. Big mistake. This battle was over before it began. Remember the Abrahamic covenant? God said, "I will bless those who bless you, and I will curse those who curse you." At this point, Goliath had a better chance of changing the course of the sun, the moon, and the stars than of killing David. This battle belonged the LORD and David was His proxy. Here is the exchange between David and Goliath in verse 44:

> "'Come to me, and I will give your flesh to the birds of the sky and the beasts of the field.' Then David said to the Philistine, 'You come to me with a sword, a spear, and a javelin, but I come to you in the name of the LORD of hosts, the God of the armies of Israel, whom you have taunted. This day the LORD will deliver you up into my hands, and I will

strike you down and remove your head from you. And I will give the dead bodies of the army of the Philistines this day to the birds of the sky and the wild beasts of the earth, that all the earth may know that there is a God in Israel, and that all this assembly may know that the LORD does not deliver by sword or by spear; for the battle is the LORD'S and He will give you into our hands.'

"Then it happened when the Philistine rose and came and drew near to meet David, that David ran quickly toward the battle line to meet the Philistine. And David put his hand into his bag and took from it a stone and slung it and struck the Philistine on his forehead. And the stone sank into his forehead, so that he fell on his face to the ground. Thus David prevailed over the Philistine with a sling and a stone, and he struck the Philistine and killed him; but there was no sword in David's hand. Then David ran and stood over the Philistine and took his sword and drew it out of its sheath and killed him, and cut off his head with it. When the Philistines saw that their champion was dead, they fled."

David kills Goliath, cuts off his head, and holds it up for both armies to see. At this point, the Israelites experienced a sudden and cataclysmic change of heart—they were invincible. They jumped over the rocks and came running toward the Philistines, waving their swords and screaming. They were going to have Philistines for breakfast and the Philistines knew it—they ran for their lives! So, what was it that turned the Israelites from wimps to warriors? The faith of one man, demonstrating what it looks like when you take God at His Word, was enough to send their morale sky-high. Consequently, the morale of their enemies was destroyed.

Here Are The Lessons

This battle is repeated every day with all the same players. Today Goliath and the Philistines come in many forms. And unfortunately, most of the good guys are still hiding behind the rocks. One example would be the atheistic school teachers and college professors who love to intimidate young uninformed students. Many of them openly mock God and ridicule Christians. In reality, people like this are hypocritical, unteachable, arrogant, ignorant, immoral bullies who love to prey upon the weak. They are giants in their own eyes, and enjoy making students feel like grasshoppers in theirs. In reality, a few well placed questions (rocks to the head) can stop their mouths every time.

Now let's look at the Israelites. Today's Israelites are rarely, if ever, seen engaged in spiritual warfare. They are content to allow someone else to fight in their stead. Knowing the world is lost, they are hiding behind the rocks watching TV as people fall into a Christless eternity. Oh sure, they believe in God—so do the demons, but you won't see them in heaven! The difference between a true believer and a make-believer is the difference between believing someone exists and knowing him personally.

Then we have the Eliabs: the hypocrites and the hypercritics. You can find them at home, next door, in the work place, and yes, even in your church. Eliab is jealous of David. Rather than focusing on the real enemy, he causes division in his own ranks. Eliabs thrive on gossip, slander, flattery, and ill will toward others. You can easily spot them. They are so self-righteous and stiff-necked they look like they've just swallowed a broomstick. They are quick to judge others, while their favorite verse is, "Thou shalt not judge thy brother."

Do you know the difference between slander and flattery? Slander is what you will say behind someone's back that you won't say to his face, and flattery is what you will say to someone's face what you won't say behind his back.

Then there's Saul. Four episodes in his life demonstrate how the fear of man played a major role in his failure as a leader.

First, at the very beginning of his rise to power, the prophet Samuel wants to present him to the people of Israel. But, Saul was nowhere to be found. So they asked the LORD where he was. Take a look at 1 Sam. 10:22:

> "Therefore they inquired further of the LORD, 'Has the man come here yet?' So the LORD said, 'Behold, he is hiding himself by the baggage.'"

Saul, the reluctant king, is *hiding* behind the baggage! Had Saul been the warrior of righteousness the Israelites needed, he would have been front and center, saying, "Here I am; send me!" Saul stood head and shoulders above everyone else in Israel. On the outside he appeared to be a warrior. On the inside he was a wimp.

Saul's second red flag came in 1 Sam. 15:24. Instead of fearing God and obeying His Word, he feared the people.

> "Then Saul said to Samuel, 'I have sinned; I have indeed transgressed the command of the LORD and your words, because I feared the people and listened to their voice.'"

Saul's third red flag came after David killed Goliath. When the Israelite army returned to Jerusalem in their triumphal entry march, all the women of the city were there to greet them. They were singing this victory chant: "Saul has slain his thousands, but David has slain his ten thousands!" Loving the praise of men, that little song caused Saul to go completely berserk. The king was so jealous of David's popularity, he thought he would never know peace until David was dead. Jealousy (selfish ambition) is covetous pride. Saul was obsessed with his own image before the people.

The fourth lesson we learn from Saul is very sad indeed. Take a look at how he died in 1 Sam. 31:4:

> "Then Saul said to his armor bearer, 'Draw your sword and pierce me through with it, lest these uncircumcised come and pierce me through and make sport of me.'"

Even in death, Saul was still possessed by the fear of man. Rather than trying to get right with God before dying, he was more concerned with what people would think, say, or do.

There are Sauls everywhere, especially in the workplace. Men in leadership not qualified to lead. They are intimidated by others, especially in their own organizations, who may have gifts and abilities. Anyone with a good idea is perceived as a threat. The only good ideas are their ideas. They love the praise of men and will crush anyone that threatens their kingdom. In some cases, they will even kill to keep it.

Then we have David. What was the difference between David and the Israelites? It's less than you think—only about 18 inches. That is how far it is from the head to the heart. Sure, the Israelites gave intellectual assent to God's existence, but David had a personal relationship with Him. David had faith, he trusted God, he relied upon

God's Word to deliver him, and he acted on his belief. What was the real difference between the Israelites and David? The Israelites believed *in* God, but David *believed* God! What you believe determines how you live.

In Acts 13:22 God said of David:

> "I have found David the son of Jesse a man after my own heart; he will do everything I want him to do."

David was on fire for God. His relationship with God left no room for the fear of man. Like David, we should all be fearless warriors for truth and righteousness. One person with a heart like David's can still change the world!

I leave you with this incredible truth about God from 2 Chr. 16:9:

> "For the eyes of the LORD move to and fro throughout the earth that He may strongly support those whose heart is completely His."

Small Group Questions

1. What was the significance of David's referring to Goliath as an "uncircumcised Philistine?"

2. What does Gal. 3:6 mean?

3. What was the difference between the Israelites and David?

4. What do you believe God wants you to learn from this story, and what do you think He wants you to do as a result?

5. Look up and discuss Heb. 4:12-13; and 2 Cor. 10:3-5. What do they mean and how do they apply?

6. Can you think of a time when you were able to encourage someone, and what effect it had on that person and on you?

7. What are the differences between David and Saul?

8. What do you admire most about David?

9. Read Acts 13:22. Why did David have favor with God?

10. Here are some verses to meditate on and discuss in small group: 2 Chron. 7:14, 16:9a; Ps. 27:1-2, Josh. 1:6-9, Jer. 29:11, Mat. 10:28, 28:19-20; Mk. 8:35-38, Rom. 1:16-25, 8:37-39; 1 Cor. 16:13, 2 Cor. 12:9, 2 Tim. 1:7-8, Eph. 6:10-18, Phil. 4:13, and Rev. 3:20.

The Righteous Are As Bold As A Lion

—∿∿∿—

The lion (*Panthera leo*) is a magnificent creature—an extremely strong, carnivorous, feline mammal. Full-grown males can weigh up 500 pounds. A lion's roar can be heard up to five miles away. Lions roar before the hunt, after the hunt, and in the morning. They have been used as symbols of power, nobility, and courage by kings, on family crests, and on national flags for thousands of years. Prv. 30:29 says:

> "The lion is mighty among beasts and does not retreat before any."

Do you know what happens when lions come to the watering hole? They're right and everybody else is wrong. Do you know how lions sleep? With both eyes closed. They do not have to worry about any other animals coming into their camp and eating them. Everybody else in the jungle has to sleep with one eye open because hungry predators can come at any time. The worst possible scenario for other animals is a pride of lions. As the king of the jungle, lions do not live in fear. In Prv. 28:1 our Creator compares His people to lions:

"The Wicked Flee When No One Pursues, But The Righteous Are Bold As A Lion."

- Lions are the only social cats; that live in groups called a pride.
- Living in prides helps the lions survive in difficult times.
- Lions are born with spots that disappear with age.
- Contrary to popular belief, both the males and females hunt.
- They often work together to capture wildebeests, zebras, antelopes and other large animals including elephants. They

will work alone when the opportunity arises and they steal kills from hyenas, wild dogs and other animals.

- The lion is known as the king of beasts because of its great strength and fighting skills. One swat from its forepaw can break a zebra's back.

Who Are The Righteous That Are Bold As Lions?

The word *righteous* in the Hebrew lexicon contains the following entries:

1. Just, right (in one's cause).
2. Just, righteous (in conduct and character).
3. Righteous (as justified and vindicated by God).
4. Right, correct.

If you are a Christian, each of these qualities have been accounted to you through Christ. Notice, the first entry is the person who is just and right in their cause. Is there any greater more noble cause than to be an Ambassador for Jesus Christ? An ambassador is the highest ranking official representing one nation to another; in this case, one kingdom to another.

As I mentioned in Chapter One, Christians have been entrusted with the ministry of reconciliation. Sin has separated man from His Creator, and the church has been given the unspeakable privilege and the great responsibility of sharing the Gospel with a world that has no hope without it. There never has been, nor shall there ever be, a greater, more noble calling. The church has been entrusted with the secrets and the mysteries of the universe.

The second lexicon entry speaks of those who are just and righteous in conduct and character. Conduct is what you do, while character is what you are, especially when you think no one is looking. As Christians we are no longer slaves to sin.

The third entry speaks of those who are justified. By virtue of Christ's death on the cross, true believers have been declared not only not guilty, but righteous.

The fourth entry speaks of those who are right, as in being correct. If you are following Jesus, you're right because He's right. See for yourself:

Buddha said, "I'm a teacher in search of truth." Jesus said, "I am the truth." Confucius said, "I never claimed to be holy." Jesus said, "Which one of you convicts Me of sin?" Mohammed said, "I do not know what Allah will do to me." Jesus said, "I am the resurrection and the life. He who believes in Me, though he die, yet shall he live." Not Buddha, Confucius, Mohammed, nor Moses ever claimed to be God. They all said 'God is this way, go this way'; and Jesus said:

> "I am the way, the truth and the life, no man comes to the Father but by Me."

Let's Look At Some Of The Heroes Of The Faith

In Exod. 11, Moses stands before the most powerful man on earth (the King of Egypt) and says:

> "…all the firstborn in the land of Egypt shall die. And all these your servants shall come down to me and bow down to me, saying, 'Get out, and all the people who follow you!' After that I will go out. Then he went out from Pharaoh in great anger.'"

In Daniel 3, Shadrach, Meshach, and Abed-Nego refuse to worship a statue. Under the penalty of death, this is what they said right to the king's face:

> "O Nebuchadnezzar, our God whom we serve is able to deliver us from the burning fiery furnace, and He will deliver us from your hand, O king. But even if He does not, we will not serve your gods."

In Daniel 6:7, all the governors had established a royal decree, that whoever petitions any god or man for thirty days, except the king, shall be cast into the den of lions. Daniel, fully aware of the king's edict:

> "…went home. And in his upper room, with his windows open toward Jerusalem, he knelt down on his knees three times that day."

Queen Esther entered the king's chambers uninvited, knowing that doing so could result in having her head removed. Her conviction, that she was doing the right thing, was greater than her fear of death. She saved untold thousands of her people from annihilation because she believed in a cause greater than her own. Her story was recorded by God to encourage us all. Esther was a woman of deep conviction.

In Acts 2:23, the Apostle Peter, filled with the Holy Spirit, said in his first recorded sermon after Pentecost:

> "This Man, delivered up by the predetermined plan and foreknowledge of God, you nailed to a cross by the hands of godless men and put Him to death. And God raised Him up again, putting an end to the agony of death, since it was impossible for Him to be held in its power."

He boldly accuses them all of murdering the Son of God and 3,000 people are saved!

If Not For Men Like William Tyndale, John Wycliffe, And Martin Luther, We Might Still Be In The Dark Ages!

It is a sad fact that in the fourth century A.D. the Roman Catholic Church hid the Bible in Latin; for over 1,000 years the Roman Catholic Church would not allow the Bible to be translated into the common languages. They forbid "laymen" from reading it, claiming that only the priests could correctly interpret the scriptures. The Roman Catholic Church persecuted and put to death those who opposed this doctrine. What a coincidence that in the middle of the fourth century A.D., when Rome hid the Bible in Latin, the world entered what is known as the "Dark Ages." This period lasted for over a thousand years. Then, in the 14th century, John Wycliffe translated the Bible into English. It was printed and distributed so the common man could once again read the Word of God. It was then that the world came out of the dark ages and into "The Age of Enlightenment!"

In referring to God's Word, the Bible, Psalm 119:105 says:

> "Thy word is a lamp to my feet, and a light to my path."

A lamp shows you where you are. The light shows you where you need to go. Unfortunately, it seems we have come full circle. As Christianity becomes criminalized once again, we are headed back into a time of deep moral and spiritual darkness. Fortunately, for believers, Jesus warned us that this is exactly what would happen prior to His second coming (see Mat. 24:25, 37-39)!

When Martin Luther discovered that salvation was by grace alone, his life became one long act of lion-hearted boldness against the false doctrines and abuses of Rome. In 1521 he appeared before a council that had the power to execute him for heresy. The prosecutor demanded, "Do you or do you not repudiate your books and the errors which they contain?" Luther replied:

> "Since then Your Majesty and your lordships desire a simple reply, I will answer without horns and without teeth. Unless I am convicted by Scripture and plain reason, I do not accept the authority of popes and councils, for they have contradicted each other—my conscience is captive to the Word of God. I cannot and I will not recant anything, for to go against conscience is neither right nor safe. Here I stand; I cannot do otherwise. God help me. Amen."

It was Luther's bold conviction that the Pope was wrong and the Bible was right that gave local governors the courage to stand up to the "Holy Roman Empire." Today, there are hundreds of millions of people who understand that we are saved by grace alone, through faith alone, through Christ alone—plus nothing! Our good works are the result of our salvation, never the cause of it. All because of the actions of one man!

A Word From Nancy Leigh Demoss

"Do not fear." Literally, "Stop being afraid." That command, "Fear not," is given over 300 times in the Scripture. You read it all the way through the Old and New Testament. I wonder if that's not because God knows that we are so prone to fear.

- We fear what we *don't* know.
- We fear what we *do* know.
- We fear things that *have* happened.
- We fear things we think *might* happen.
- We fear things that *are* happening.
- We fear things we think *might* happen but *never* do.

The word means to be struck with fear or seized with alarm, and you know how fear can be paralyzing. It makes you want to run, or it can make you just stand dead still in your tracks. Whichever is your inclination, God's Word says, don't be afraid. Don't be seized with alarm. Don't be struck with fear. Don't be put to flight."[1]

As Christians, we should be the most loving, joyful, kind, good, gentle, faithful, forgiving, blessed, bold, bubbling-over, charged-up, cheerful, confident, content, encouraging, enraptured, energized, excited, exuberant, exhilarated, ecstatic, elated, enthusiastic, fun-loving, festive, fearless, God- fearing, good-humored, good-natured, generous, glad, gracious, gratified, happy, hospitable, humble, holy, inspiring, jubilant, optimistic, on-fire, peaceful, patient, pleased, prosperous, positive, passionate, proper, satisfied, self-controlled, sunny, smiling, successful, tickled, truthful, vibrant, vivacious, Holy Spirit-filled people on the planet!

In Closing

In *The Patriot*, a movie starring Mel Gibson, there is a scene containing a short speech that I love. The movie tells the story of the War of Independence in 1776. The American colonies wanted to secede from England to begin a sovereign American nation. In this scene Corporal Gabriel Martin, the son of Captain Benjamin Martin (played by Mel Gibson), is recruiting men to join the South Carolina Militia. He walks into a church service being held in honor of a small group of men who were murdered by British troops. He politely asks for permission to speak. Here is the scene:

> "Reverend, with your permission, I would like to make an announcement." "Young man, this is a house of God." "I understand that, Reverend, I apologize. The South Carolina Militia is being called up. I'm here to enlist every man willing." Reverend: "Son, we are here to pray for the men hanging outside." Gabriel: "Yes, pray for them, but honor them by taking up arms with us." A church member stands up: "And, bring more suffering to this town? If King George can hang those men, our friends, he can hang any one of us." A courageous young lady stands to her feet: "Den Scott, barely a week ago I heard you rail for two hours about independence. Mr. Hartwig, how many times have I heard you speak of freedom at my father's table? Half the men in this church, including you, father, and you, Reverend, (the violins begin playing in the background) are as ardent patriots as I. Will

you now, when you are needed most, stop only at words? Is that the sort of men you are? I ask only that you act upon the beliefs of which you have so strongly spoken, and in which you so strongly believe." After a long pause, the music now begins playing *The Patriot's* theme. Gabriel asks, "Who is with us?" Now, the men begin looking at each other and then their families. Slowly, one man stands up, then another, then another, and before long every eligible man in the room is standing and looking at Gabriel. It's a moving scene, because these men were willing to give up everything, even their families, to join the fight for civil liberty!

Millions of people have given their lives fighting for their country. How much more should we be willing to give our lives for the cause of Christ? I ask you now, will you, when you are needed most, stop only at words? Is that the sort of person you are? I ask only that you act upon the beliefs of which you have so strongly spoken, and in which you so strongly believe.

"I solemnly charge you in the presence of God and of Christ Jesus, who is to judge the living and the dead, and by His appearing and His kingdom: preach the word; be ready in season and out of season; reprove, rebuke, exhort, with great patience and instruction." 2 Tim. 4:1-2

Be as bold as a lion!

Small Group Questions

1. What did Jesus mean by, "I have overcome the world?"

2. For people to be truly satisfied they need three things: something to do, something to hope for, and someone to love and be loved by. How are all three of these needs fulfilled in Christ? Can you show the Bible verses to support each answer?

3. What are the characteristics that make Christians bold as lions?

4. What is the Christian's ultimate purpose in life? Check your answers against Ecc. 12:13-14.

5. How does being just and right in character make us as confident as a lion?

6. How and why are we justified by God? Check Rom. 5:1, 5:9.

7. The last entry speaks of those who are right, meaning correct. How do we know we are right?

8. What is the difference between conduct and character?

9. How can God legally forgive a sinful person without compromising His justice?

10. How do we know God loves us? Check John 3:16 and Rom. 5:8.

The Amazing Spiritual Secrets Of Salt And Light

—ɯ—

"You are the salt of the earth; but if the salt has become taste-less, how will it be made salty again. It is good for nothing anymore, except to be thrown out and trampled under foot by men" Matthew 5:13.

Speaking figuratively, Jesus tells us that Christians are the "salt of the earth and the light of the world." Salt is an amazing substance. It is made up of two elements, sodium and chlorine. Sodium and chlorine by themselves are extremely reactive substances. Sodium is so unstable that it can burst into flame when exposed to water. Chlorine is a lethal gas. Put the two together and you have simple table salt which is absolutely essential to all of life on planet earth!

The oceans contain an estimated 40 million, billion tons of salt. If the oceans evaporated, it is estimated that there would be enough salt to cover all of Great Britain to a depth of 50 miles. The ocean acts like a giant washing machine. The rain washes pollutants found in the air and in the earth down into the rivers which empty into the oceans. The gravitational pull from the moon causes the tides to come in and go out. The wind causes the waves, and you get the washing machine effect. Approximately 1.9% of the mass of seawater contains chloride ions. Chlorine is a powerful oxidant and is used in bleaching and disinfectants.

The heat from the sun (93 million miles away) causes tiny droplets of water to evaporate, but the salt stays in the ocean. The fresh water rises to the clouds, the clouds produce rain, and the hydrologic cycle begins all over again. As an interesting side note, the hydrologic cycle is described perfectly in Job, which many theologians believe to be the oldest book in the Bible!

"He [God] draws up the drops of water; they distill rain from the mist, which the clouds pour down, they drip upon man abundantly" Job 36:27-28.

"He binds up the waters in his thick clouds; and the cloud is not torn under them" Job 26:8. This verse speaks of the formation of clouds by condensation.

Salt Is Also Essential For Human Life!

Your body needs four ounces of salt. Salt assists in the digestion of food, and without it your heart won't beat. It is salt that makes muscles contract that causes the blood to flow. It is essential for the transmission of nerve impulses to and from the brain. Interestingly, the human body does not produce either sodium or chloride, so it must be ingested from an external source. Salt comes from water and it's mined from the earth. It corrodes metal, but it preserves food. It holds water, but it makes you thirsty. Salt is hard, but it softens water.

Seven Spiritual Secrets Of Salt

#1. Salt Preserves

Using salt was an ancient preservation technique. In the Bible days they did not have the luxury of electricity, or the convenience of re-frigerator-freezers. So, meat was heavily salted to keep it from putre-fying. Salted meat could last for up to four months. Salt removes the moisture that bacteria need to survive.

In the same way, the church is the salt that preserves this world from rotting in sin. As sin and corruption increase, so the foundation of society weakens. Today, much our political and judicial system is based on the philosophy that the best liar wins, but not for long. Prv. 21:6 says:

> "Getting treasures by a lying tongue is the fleeting fantasy of those who seek death."

Can you imagine what would happen to our world if everybody always told the truth, and if everybody stopped stealing tomorrow? Gibbon, in his classic work entitled: *The Decline and Fall of the Roman Empire*, listed five reasons for its demise. One was the decadence of the people.

Every time someone receives Christ the effect is the same. They are no longer dead in trespasses and sins, but alive in Christ. The old things pass away, and he or she becomes a new creature in Christ. Every person you lead to the LORD adds salt to our decaying world, and the process of decay is slowed.

#2. Salt Burns

Do you know what happens if you get salt in an open wound? You'll be running for water because salt burns! When you put salt on an open wound it stimulates pain-sensing neurons in much the same way a jalapeño pepper burns your tongue.

John 16:8 says: "When He the Holy Spirit comes, He will convict the world of sin, righteousness and judgment." The word *convict* means: to expose the hidden things and to chastise in a moral sense. Just as light exposes darkness, the Christian brings conviction of sin—that burns our pride.

#3. Salt Heals

Salt is a powerful antiseptic. It kills micro-organisms and germs on contact. If you have a sore throat, for example, gargling with warm salt water brings noticeable relief almost instantly. The blood of Jesus Christ is the only healing agent there is for sin. In 1 Peter 2:24, the Bible says:

> "…and He Himself bore our sins in His body on the cross, that we might die to sin and live to righteousness; for by His wounds you were healed."

This is a reference to a passage out of the 53rd chapter of Isaiah. The Bible says that it is only by the blood sacrifice of Jesus Christ that the effect of sin (which is eternal separation from God) can be healed. Christians have been entrusted by God to bring this message of healing to a lost and dying world.

Salty Christians know their Bibles well enough that when people need help, be it prayer or spiritual guidance, we are agents of mental, physical, and spiritual healing.

#4. Salt Seasons

Salt adds flavor to bland food. That is what happens when Jesus comes into your life. The first recorded miracle Jesus performed is in John chapter two. Jesus turned water into wine at a wedding. In His un-worldliness, Jesus was not indifferent or unsociable. Jesus engaged "sinners."

The point of God's miracle at this wedding reveals a wonderful spiritual truth. When Christ shows up at the party of your life, a bland and boring life becomes a beautiful, fruitful life. It's the difference between serving tepid water and the finest wine at your wedding. When Christ shows up in your life the black and white becomes living color. The ordinary becomes the extraordinary. The caterpillar becomes a butterfly!

#5. Salt Penetrates

One tablespoon of salt will thoroughly penetrate an entire gallon of water. It is one of the few major compounds that dissolve very well in hot or cold water. Similarly, there are two best times to share the Gospel—in season and out of season.

Just as salt penetrates, so we are to penetrate the culture with the Gospel of Jesus Christ. Isn't that exactly what the disciples of Jesus did? A spoonful of disciples, 12 to be exact, were credited with "turning the world upside down" with the Gospel. Today, 2.5 billion people claim Christ as their Savior!

#6. Salt Creates Thirst

Ocean water contains seven times more salt than the human body can safely ingest. A person becomes dehydrated by drinking it because the kidneys demand extra water to flush out the overload of salt. The more salt water someone drinks, the thirstier he becomes. He actually dies of dehydration.

When people try to find satisfaction in sin, they become like the man trying to satisfy his thirst by drinking salt water. The lust of the flesh is never satisfied! We search desperately for satisfaction. We see something that looks like what we want. We don't realize, however, that it is precisely the opposite of what we really need. If you are seeking satisfaction in all the wrong places, you may get what you want, but you're not going to like what you get. Sin produces only pain and death.

As salty Christians, our lives should be filled with love, joy, peace, patience, kindness, goodness, faithfulness, gentleness and self-control. This is attractive to people who are hungry for spiritual truth. In that sense, Christ in us should create a thirst in others for what we have.

#7. Salt Conducts Electricity

If you have ever taken high school chemistry you're familiar with this simple experiment. Two ends of an electrical wire are attached to a light bulb and a power source. The other ends are submerged into a glass of water. Because pure water alone is not conductive, the bulb does not light up. But when we add a little salt to the water, the bulb starts to glow. As Spirit-filled Christians, we are to be conduits of God's power and God's love, bringing light and life to those around us.

Now, Let's Look At The Application In Matt 5:13:

"You are the salt of the earth; but if the salt loses its flavor, how will it be made salty again? It is good for nothing anymore, except to be thrown out and trampled under foot by men."

This is a fascinating verse that provides an interesting problem. Strictly speaking, sodium chloride is a stable compound. It has an indefinite shelf life. It does not lose its flavor. But wait a minute, Christ's illustrations were perfect. *He created salt.* Is there a mistake in the Bible? The problem is in the translation from the original Greek language into English. The words translated "become tasteless" according to the Greek dictionary also meant…"to cause something to lose the purpose for which it was designed." Now, this verse makes perfect sense. With all we have learned about salt, here is the point:

Salt Is An Amazing Compound But It Doesn't Do Anything Until It Comes Into Direct Contact With Another Substance!

If you believe yourself to be a Christian, but you are not emulating the characteristics of salt, Jesus says you are not serving the purpose for which you were created. Sadly, it also means you are good for nothing except to be thrown out.

The Amazing Spiritual Secrets Of Light

"You are the light of the world. A city set on a hill cannot be hidden. Nor do men light a lamp, and put it under the peck-measure, but on the lampstand; and it gives light to all who are in the house. Let your light shine before men in such a way that they may see your good works, and glorify your Father who is in heaven" Mat. 5:14-16.

Light is an amazing phenomenon that is still not completely understood by science. We may never completely understand what light is. Why do I say that? In 1 John 1:5 the Bible says:

"God Is Light."

When Albert Einstein published his paper on the Theory of Relativity in 1910, his quest began by trying to answer the question, "What is light?" Einstein's research led to the discovery of the mathematical equation $E=MC^2$. That is, energy equals mass, times the speed of light, squared.

According to Einstein, achieving the speed of light (186,000 miles per second), is no small task. As you go faster and faster the need for power grows exponentially. Are you ready for this? According to Einstein, in order to achieve the speed of light you would literally need *unlimited power*. This again fits the biblical model perfectly. The Bible assures us that God is light, and He alone is omnipotent!

Light is a form of energy. It is the fastest phenomenon that we know of in the universe. It can be as harmless as a 25 watt light bulb, as deadly as a CO_2 laser beam (which cuts the hardest steel like butter), or as in God's case, omnipotent.

Einstein proved that time, space, and matter were not only related, but had a beginning. This again fits the biblical model perfectly. The very first verse in the Bible says:

"In the beginning God created the heavens and the earth."

In the beginning (that's time), God created (that's energy) the heavens (that's space) and the earth (that's matter). Coincidence? Here is another one.

White light appears colorless. But, if you shine it through a prism you see a brilliant display of the seven primary colors—red, yellow, orange, green, blue, indigo, and purple. The colors come from a refraction of the different wavelengths of light. Interesting that Revelation 4:5 speaks of the seven spirits of God.

Here is one more interesting "coincidence" involving God and light.

- First, we know that there is invisible light such as infrared, ultraviolet, X-ray, gamma ray, and radio waves.

- Second, there is visible light such as light from the sun or a light bulb.

- Third, the heat that is associated with light.

The relationship between heat and light is not yet fully understood by science. However, the three characteristics of light listed above provide an interesting similarity to what the Bible reveals about the nature of God. In 1 Timothy 1:17 the Bible says God the Father is invisible:

> "Now to the King eternal, immortal, invisible, the only God, be honor and glory forever and ever."

And, in John 4:24 we read:

> "God is spirit and those who worship Him must worship in spirit and in truth."

Then we have John 1:1 and 1:14, which say that God the Son is visible:

> "In the beginning was the Word, and the Word was with God, and the Word was God."

> "And the Word became flesh, and dwelt among us, and we beheld His glory, glory as of the only begotten from the Father, full of grace and truth."

And in 1 John 1:1, speaking of Jesus, we read:

"What was from the beginning, what we have heard, what we have seen with our eyes, what we beheld and our hands handled, concerning the Word of Life."

Another great verse is Col. 1:15 which tells us that Jesus Christ is the physical manifestation of the invisible God!

Finally, speaking of the Holy Spirit, the third person of the Trinity, there is an association with fire (light and heat) in Mat. 3:11:

"As for me, I baptize you with water for repentance, but He who is coming after me is mightier than I, and I am not fit to remove His sandals; He will baptize you with the Holy Spirit and fire."

Here is another verse that associates the Holy Spirit with fire from Acts 2:3-4:

"And there appeared to them tongues as of fire distributing themselves, and they rested on each one of them. And they were all filled with the Holy Spirit and began to speak with other tongues, as the Spirit was giving them utterance."

Now Let's Revisit Matthew 5:14-16:

"You are the light of the world. A city that is set on a hill cannot be hidden. Nor do they light a lamp and put it under a basket, but on a lampstand, and it gives light to all who are in the house. Let your light so shine before men, that they may see your good works and glorify your Father in heaven."

When you tour some of the great caves in America, often the tour guide will take you down to where there is no light. It is so dark you can't see your hand in front of your face. The darkness is so thick, you can almost feel it. Then the guide lights a match, and the whole cave lights up. If you could distill all the darkness in the universe, and place it in a bottle, one match has enough candle power to dispel that darkness. Light is infinitely more powerful than darkness. In the Bible, light and darkness are used as metaphors for good and evil.

Like salt, a light that does not work is good for nothing but to be thrown out. Whether you are a 25 watt light bulb or a CO_2 laser beam, God's gifts of light and life are to be used to help others find their way. If you have failed, I have good news.

It Is Not Too Late To Start Living Right

I received a call one day from an organization known as Inner City Impact in Chicago. The man asked me if I would be interested in addressing their youth group at a weekend retreat up in Wisconsin. I said, "I would love to address your youth group. What would you like me to teach on?" The answer was, "sexual purity." I gulped, and asked what age group they were and the answer was, "high school." My heart sank as I hung up the phone. I remember thinking to myself, *I would much rather be locked up in a maximum security prison and preach on the love of God, than face these young people and try to convince them that purity is the best way to go.*

Please don't misunderstand. I believe with all my heart that this is one of the most critical issues of our day, and it needs to be addressed. My problem was, I had never preached on that particular subject to that particular age group before, and I don't like to preach unless I have something compelling to say. Fortunately, I had three months to prepare.

At the retreat, I had approximately 50 girls on my left, and 50 boys on my right. I asked the girls, "How would you like to know the three secrets that will make you the most eligible girl in your entire neighborhood for marriage?" I was met with a resounding, "Yes!" I said, "A real man, a good man, will be looking for three things in a wife: First, someone he can respect; second, someone who is special; and third, someone who is a challenge. Now watch and listen very carefully."

I walked over to the boys and said, "Gentlemen, if you had the opportunity to marry one of two women, both equally beautiful, both equally talented, both equally gifted, and both with dynamic personalities—in fact, they're identical twins. The only difference between the two is, one of them has had multiple sexual partners, and the other one is a virgin. How many will take the virgin? Raise your hands." Without hesitation, *all of them smiled* and raised their hands. I said, "Gentlemen, keep your hands right where they are!" I walked back over to the girls and said, "Ladies, I don't care what they're telling you in the back seat of the car on Saturday night, take a good look at 'em now, because there's the naked truth!" I could see many of them turning their heads like curious puppies, obviously thinking to themselves, "Wow, there's a revolutionary concept. I never thought of that before."

I went on to say, "For those of you who are still virgins, just remember that you can always become like the girls who are not, but they can never become like you. As for those who have lost their virginity, I have some good news for you. It's never too late to start living right. The next best thing is 'secondary virginity.' You can decide today to remain celibate. If you have to wait one, two, five, or ten years for the right man to come along, and you tell him you have been waiting for him all that time, I guarantee you he will think you are someone he can respect, you are special, and you are a challenge."[1] They *all* applauded! They understood the point. It is not too late to start living right.

If you have never shared your faith with others, the same principle applies. It is not too late to start. However, the day is coming, burning like a furnace when it will be too late. Consider Revelation 19:7: "Let us rejoice and be glad and give the glory to Him, for the marriage of the Lamb has come and His bride has made herself ready."

Jesus is the Lamb and the church is His bride. Someday soon, those who love Him will be invited to the marriage supper when Christ and His church will be united forever in heaven. Have you made yourself ready? Do you know Jesus and does He know you? When a young lady gets engaged to be married, does she hide her engagement ring and keep her love a secret, or does she introduce him to her family and friends and invite them all to the wedding? How many people have you invited to the wedding?

Small Group Questions

1. Read Dan. 12:3, Mat. 5:19 and 1 Pet. 4:14. How is sharing the Gospel with someone a win-win situation?

2. How would you paraphrase Mat. 6:33?

3. Read Mat. 5:13-16. What do you think Jesus means by this verse?

4. Have you ever shared your faith with an unbeliever? If not, why not?

5. Figuratively speaking, why are Christians compared to salt and light?

6. Read Mark 8:38. What does it mean? How does it apply to us?

7. What is the purpose you were created serve?

8. Figuratively speaking, name three kinds of fruit God enjoys.

9. How would you describe yourself? Are you a 10 watt bulb about to burn out? Are you 100 watts, 1,000 watts, or are you a CO2 laser beam melting everything in its path?

10. How would those who know you best describe your flavor—sugar, salt, pepper, horseradish, tepid water, or fine wine?

CHAPTER SEVEN

There Are Two Kinds Of People In The World: Those Who Think They Can, And Those Who Think They Can't, And They're Both Right

—⟋𝕞⟍—

I love knowing that my attitude, which is something I choose in any given situation and in life, can make the difference between success and failure. The following story provides a great illustration of this truth.

When I was 15 years old, I was barely in high school. You've heard of people who graduate Summa Cum Laude and Magna Cum Laude? When I graduated it was, "Thank you Laude!" Anyway, I convinced the Superintendent of Public Schools that we needed a special program for the kids who thought that most of what they were teaching was irrelevant. Oh, I understood why we needed reading, writing, and arithmetic, but there were some of us who needed more. We wanted to know about life and how to succeed. The Superintendent agreed. He convinced the school board, and they appropriated $110,000 for an experimental program to begin the following year. This was back in the late 60's.

The following school year, 12 hand-picked students and two teachers (who also thought school could offer more) were moved into a small unused building owned by the park district. The program was originally called S.C.C. for Self-Contained Classroom. Today it's called STEP. The teachers were both believers, outdoor types, and both had a passion for life and for leadership.

One day they told us that they were going to select two or three students to become "Junior Leaders." They were to become role models of leadership and excellence to the rest of the class. They would be given extra responsibilities and *extra privileges*. In order to become a Junior Leader candidates would need to pass a rigorous test, and only the serious need apply. One of the principles that these men were trying to teach us was that hard work and perseverance were essential elements of successful living. These were character traits we needed if we wanted to achieve great things in life. Since I was the founder of the program, it seemed only fitting to me that I should step up to the plate first to see if I had what it took.

When the "test day" arrived, the meeting consisted of the two teachers (our nick names for them were "Boomer," and "Porky"), our bus driver, and me. They asked me a battery of questions mainly having to do with character and what I might do in certain hypothetical situations. When the oral examination was over, they huddled as if to be comparing notes to decide whether or not I had passed. While I was nervously waiting for their answer, when they turned to me they appeared solemn. Boomer looked at me and said, "I'm sorry, but you failed." My eyes hit the floor with disappointment, which was followed by a moment of silence. Then, in a somber tone Boomer asked:

"What are you going to do now?"

I thought for a moment, I looked up and said, "I'm going to try again." Instantly their countenance changed. They smiled as all six of their eyes lit up simultaneously. Boomer reached his hand out to shake mine. With joy in his face and pride in his voice, he said, "YOU PASSED!!!" "I did?" "Yes!" "But, you said…" "That was all part of the test. We wanted to see how you would respond to failure. Would you give up, or try again?" By then, I was smiling! I looked at the other two men in disbelief, and they were smiling and nodding their heads in the affirmative. Wow. I passed. I'm a Junior Leader!

That's Only Half Of The Story

I was strictly forbidden to tell anyone else in the class how the test worked, or it would obviously ruin the whole thing. When the next candidate took the test, I was also sitting on the search committee since I was now in leadership. It was a friend of mine who decided to take the test. He went through basically the same questions I did. When it was over, we told him he failed and waited to see how he would respond. When we asked him the closing question, "What are you going to do now?" he started cursing us like a drunken sailor. He told us what we could do with our Junior Leader program in no uncertain terms. His true character had been revealed. Clearly, at this point in his life, he was not Junior Leader material. So, how does this story apply to you?

All Of Life Is A Test

"And there is no creature hidden from His sight, but all things are naked and open to the eyes of Him to whom we must give account" Hebrews 4:13.

God created the heavens and the earth, which reveal his eternal power and divine nature. Then He wrote a book that only He could write. Finally, God wrote the moral law on every man's heart so we would know the difference between right and wrong. In this light, there is no excuse for atheism.

Obviously, my hope is that you adopt an attitude of gratitude and get involved. Your attitude can make all the difference. Here is a great quote by Charles Swindoll on attitude:

"The longer I live, the more I realize the impact of attitude on life. Attitude to me is more important than facts. It is more important than the past, than education, than money, than circumstances, than failures, than successes, than what other people think or say or do. It is more important than appearance, giftedness, or skill. It will make or break a company…a church…a home. The remarkable thing is we have a choice every day regarding the attitude we will embrace for that day. We cannot change the inevitable. The only thing we can do is play on the one string we have, and that is our attitude. I am convinced that life is 10% what happens to me and 90% how I react to it. And so it is with you … we are in charge of our attitudes."

Examples We Can Learn From

Matthew Henry was an 18th century preacher, pastor, and a prolific writer. His Bible commentaries are still in print today. As Pastor Henry was walking to church one Sunday morning he was robbed!

He did not mention the incident in his sermon that morning. It was only discovered in his memoirs after his death. This is what he wrote:

"I was robbed on my way to church this morning, and I thanked God for four things:

1. I only had very little;
2. I had never been robbed before;
3. The thief took my wallet and not my life;
4. And, I was the one robbed and not the robber!

Here Is An Important Public Service Announcment About Attitude From Elizabeth Elliot

"The very experiences that we would see as overwhelming are the very things that Paul claims helped him learn the secret of peace and contentment. Everything about which we are tempted to complain may be the very instrument whereby the Potter intends to shape His clay into the image of His Son—a headache, an insult, a long line at the check-out, someone's rudeness or failure to say thank you, misunderstanding, disappointment, interruption. As Amy Carmichael said, 'See in it a chance to die,' meaning a chance to leave self behind and say yes to the will of God, to be 'conformable unto His death.'"

Who Are "They" Anyway?

"They" dismissed her from drama school with a note that read, "Wasting her time; she's too shy to put her best foot forward." Her name? Lucille Ball.

Turned down by the Decca Recording Company, "they" said, "We don't like their sound and guitar music is on the way out." Whom did they turn down? The Beatles.

"They" cut him from the high school basketball team. He went home, locked himself in his room, and cried. Who was it "they" cut from the team? Michael Jordan.

"They" told him he was too stupid to learn anything. He should go into a field where he might succeed due to his pleasant personality. Who was this child who was "too stupid to learn anything?" Thomas Edison.

"They" fired him from a newspaper because they said he lacked imagination and had no original ideas. Who was it? Walt Disney.

"They" told Ben Hogan he would never walk again due to an auto accident. He went on to become a championship golfer.

"They" told Ann Sullivan her mission was impossible. Refusing to give up, Ann taught a deaf and dumb girl to communicate through sign language, thus saving her from a cold, closed, institutionalized life. That girls name was Helen Keller.

Col. Sanders didn't start his first Kentucky Fried Chicken until he was 69 years old. Today, the franchise is worldwide.

Grandma Moses didn't start painting until she was 75. She lived to be 101. Her paintings became famous.

Beethoven was almost totally deaf and burdened with sorrow when he produced his greatest works.

Bread And Water Become Toast And Tea

In merry old 18th century England, John Bunyan was locked in Bedford Prison for his constant preaching of the Gospel. While there, they brought him a meal—bread and water. He looked at the meal, then up to heaven, and said to God, "All this and heaven too?" He went on to write *Pilgrim's Progress,* one of the best selling books of all time…while in prison.

Hudson Taylor, the great missionary to China, became deathly ill during the peak of his ministry with the China Inland Mission. At the same time the Chinese government was exerting maximum pressure on him to close the mission. It was precisely then that he wrote in his journal:

"The future is as bright as are the promises of God."

Anytime you feel like quitting, remember this man: He failed in business in '31. He ran as a state legislator and lost in '32. He tried business again in '33 and failed again. His sweetheart died in '35. He had a nervous breakdown in '36. He ran for State Elector in '40 after he regained his health. He was defeated for Congress in '43, defeated again for Congress in '48. He was defeated again when he ran for the Senate in '55 and defeated for the Vice Presidency of the United

States in '56. He ran for the Senate again in '58 and lost again. He kept on trying until at last in 1860, after 30 years of rejection, Abraham Lincoln was elected the 16th President of the United States.

Classic Attitudes Of Humility From Scripture:

"Though the fig tree should not blossom, and there be no fruit on the vines, though the yield of the olive should fail, and the fields produce no food, though the flock should be cut off from the fold, and there be no cattle in the stalls, yet I will exult in the LORD; I will rejoice in the God of my salvation" Hab. 3:17-18.

Job is perhaps the greatest illustration of all time of a man who refused to adopt a bad attitude in the face of incredible suffering through no fault of his own. In fact, the Bible says he was a righteous and blameless man before God. After all was said and done, Job passed the test with flying colors. God allowed Satan to kill his children, destroy his vast wealth, and to afflict him with extremely painful boils from the top of his head to the tips of his toes. Here is Job's attitude toward God:

"Though He slay me yet will I praise Him!"

One of the many things that are unique to Christianity is the fact that humility is exalted as a virtue. Humility is associated with God and godliness. In the eyes of the world, humility is viewed as a weakness. But not according to Jesus. He said:

"Take My yoke upon you, and learn from Me, for I am gentle and humble in heart; and you shall find rest for your souls."

The Definition Of *Humility*

"The prominence it (humility) gained in Christian thought indicates the new conception of man in relation to God, to himself, and to his fellow man, which is unique to Christianity. It by no means implies slavishness or servility; nor is it inconsistent with a right estimate of oneself, one's gifts, and calling of God, or with proper self-assertion when called for.

"But the habitual frame of mind of a child of God is that of one who feels not only that he owes all his natural gifts, etc., to God, but that he has been the object of undeserved redeeming love, and who regards himself as being not his own, but God's in Christ. He cannot exalt himself, for he knows that he has nothing of himself. The humble mind is thus at the root of all other graces and virtue. Self-exaltation spoils everything." [1]

According to Paul, there can be no love without humility. In 1 Cor. 13:4, Paul said, "love is not proud." The first of the Beatitudes given by Jesus was to "the poor in spirit" (Mt. 5:3), and in Mat. 5:5 it is "the meek" who "inherit the earth." Moses was called the "meekest man on earth." According to the Bible, humility is the way to true greatness. In Mat. 18:2-4, Jesus said:

> "And He called a child to Himself and set him before them, and said, 'Truly I say to you, unless you are converted and become like children, you shall not enter the kingdom of heaven. Whoever then humbles himself as this child, he is the greatest in the kingdom of heaven.'"

12 Action Steps To Cultivate The Heart Attitude That God Will Bless

1. Humility is how God defines greatness.

Mark 10:43: "But it is not so among you, but whoever wishes to become great among you shall be your servant; and whoever wishes to be first among you shall be slave of all."

2. Understand that humility is God's will for you.

Micah 6:8: "He has told you, O man, what is good; and what does the LORD require of you but to do justice, to love kindness, and to walk humbly with your God?"

3. God hates pride—we should too.

Prv. 16:5: "Everyone who is proud in heart is an abomination to the LORD; assuredly, he will not be unpunished."

1 Pet. 5:5: "You younger men, likewise, be subject to your elders; and all of you, clothe yourselves with humility to-

ward one another, for God is opposed to the proud, but gives grace to the humble."

4. Confess the sin of pride to God and seek His resurrection power to overcome it.

1 Jn. 1:9: "If we confess our sins, He is faithful and righteous to forgive us our sins and to cleanse us from all unrighteousness."

Phil. 3:10-11: "That I may know Him, and the power of His resurrection and the fellowship of His sufferings, being conformed to His death; in order that I may attain to the resurrection from the dead."

5. Realize that everything you have is a gift from God.

1 Cor. 4:7: "For who regards you as superior? And what do you have that you did not receive? But if you did receive it, why do you boast as if you had not received it?"

6. Remember, Jesus was characterized by humility.

John 13:14: "If I then, the Lord and the Teacher, washed your feet, you also ought to wash one another's feet."

7. God dwells with and revives (gives life) to the humble.

Isaiah 57:15: "For thus says the high and exalted One who lives forever, whose name is Holy, 'I dwell on a high and holy place, and also with the contrite and lowly of spirit in order to revive the spirit of the lowly and to revive the heart of the contrite.'"

8. Know this: the world does not have the answer.

1 Jn. 2:16-17: "For all that is in the world, the lust of the flesh and the lust of the eyes and the boastful pride of life, is not from the Father, but is from the world. And the world is passing away, and also its lusts; but the one who does the will of God abides forever."

Look at the lives of the movie stars and the rock stars. They think they have it all—fame, fortune, food, fun, fashion, football, and fornication. The vast majority of them also have deep depression, drug and alcohol dependencies, drug overdoses, domestic violence, divorces by the dozen, deadly accidents, and deaths by suicide. Elvis and Michael were two of the most pathetic cases in history.

Lottery winners in many ways are actually lottery losers. I found a study that was done on them to see what happened after they won their millions. Initially it was fun, but when the honeymoon ended, the party crashed. After seeing the effect it had on their lives, I could not find one who said, "Winning the lottery was the greatest thing that ever happened to me." In fact, almost all of them said just the opposite!

9. Learn the joy of giving and serving.

Prv. 11:25: "The generous man will be prosperous, and he who waters will himself be watered."

Acts 20:35: "In everything I showed you that by working hard in this manner you must help the weak and remember the words of the Lord Jesus, that He Himself said, 'It is more blessed to give than to receive.'"

10. Invite and accept constructive criticism graciously.

Prv. 10:17: "He is on the path of life who heeds instruction, but he who forsakes reproof goes astray."

Prv. 12:1: "Whoever loves discipline loves knowledge, but he who hates reproof is stupid."

11. Jesus said humility is something that is learned.

Mat. 11:29: "Take My yoke upon you, and learn from Me, for I am gentle and humble in heart; and you shall find rest for your souls."

12. Measure yourself against Ex. 20:1-19 and 1 Cor. 13:1-7.

This should put pride and humility in a new light.

Small Group Questions

1. Read 1 Cor. 13:1-7 to the group. How do you measure up? What effect should this have on you?

2. What do you think God wants us to learn from Job?

3. Define the word *attitude*. What are the causes and effects of our attitudes?

4. What is God's position on complaining? Why?

5. Read Matthew 18:3-4. What are some of the characteristics of children that Jesus is looking for in us?

6. What makes humility so attractive?

7. What is pride and why does God hate it?

8. What was the most meaningful lesson for you personally in this chapter?

9. In what ways did Jesus humble Himself? Why did Jesus humble Himself?

10. Read and discuss each of the 12 action steps to growing in humility. Which ones apply most to you, and why?

CHAPTER EIGHT

How To Be Delivered From The Fear Of Man

—⟪⟫—

N one of us are immune from the fear of man. The Apostles themselves were not exempt. They were eyewitnesses of God's majesty, His power, and His glory. They too experienced the power of the world, the flesh, and the devil—the three sources from which the fear of man derives its power.

Deliverance from the guilt and the power of sin is a work of grace. A work of grace is something only God can do. Paradoxically, your part must be factored in. God's work is done in you and *through you* as you learn to trust in, rely upon, and submit to Him. This idea is found in Gal. 5:22 where it says, "The fruit of the Spirit… is self-control." (Also see Ezek. 22:30.)

The word *grace* in English is (khar'-ece) in Greek. Most Bible teachers will tell you that grace means "unmerited favor," and it does. But God's grace is much more than that. Here is the best definition of grace I have found:

1. Grace is the divine influence upon the heart and its reflection in the life including gratitude, good will, loving-kindness, and favor. It is used of the merciful kindness of God, by which He exerts His holy influence upon souls, turning them to Christ; keeping, strengthening, and increasing them in faith, knowledge, and affection. Grace kindles the exercise of Christian virtue and moral excellence.

2. The spiritual condition of one governed by the power of divine grace.

Jesus Christ Is Grace Personified

"For the grace of God has appeared, bringing salvation to all men, instructing us to deny ungodliness and worldly desires and to live sensibly, righteously and godly in the present age, looking for the blessed hope and the appearing of the glory of our great God and Savior, Christ Jesus; who gave Himself for us, that He might redeem us from every lawless deed and purify for Himself a people for His own possession, zealous for good deeds" (Titus 2:11-14).

How can I be set free from the fear of man?

Here Are Seven Action Steps To Get You There

Action Step #1: Pray.

The first time I ever read Matthew 10:32-33, I was deeply convicted. These are the words of Jesus:

> "Everyone therefore who shall confess Me before men, I will also confess him before My Father who is in heaven. But whoever shall deny Me before men, I will also deny him before My Father who is in heaven."

I knew exactly what He meant, and I was totally blown away by it. Jesus was saying in no uncertain terms, "If you are sincere about following Me, there is no such thing as walking the fence. You are either for Me or you are against Me. You are either part of the problem or you are part of the solution. You are either an asset or you are a liability. In His own words, "You either gather with Me or you scatter!"

I knew that if I became a fully-devoted follower of the Lord Jesus Christ, I would have to tell my family and friends about Jesus. I was afraid of being called a "Jesus freak" or a "religious fanatic." So, I prayed, "LORD, if you will take that fear of man away from me, I will never miss an opportunity to speak for You. Wherever I am, whatever I am doing, if I feel Your elbow in my ribs, I'll say whatever You want me to say to whomever You want me to say it." I didn't know at the time that Scripture also said in 1 John 5:14-15:

> "And this is the confidence which we have before Him, that, if we ask anything according to His will, He hears us. And if we know that He hears us in whatever we ask, we know that we have the requests which we have asked from Him."

I asked for something that was according to God's will, and I meant it. As you may have guessed by reading this book, I am no longer ashamed of the Gospel. In Rom. 1:16 Paul said:

> "For I am not ashamed of the Gospel, for it is the power of God for salvation to everyone who believes, to the Jew first and also to the Greek."

As far as your part is concerned, when it comes to prayer, the condition of your heart is the difference between success and failure. You must be sincere. The English word *sincere* comes from two Latin words meaning "pure" and "without wax." In ancient times, potters would sometimes have their pottery crack during the drying process. Some unscrupulous potters, rather than throwing the flawed piece away, would fill in the cracks with wax and paint over it. A shrewd buyer, aware of this practice, also knew that if you held the finished piece up to the sun, the light from the sun would expose the flaws. The potter would cry, "Sincere, sincere!" Meaning, "without wax." If you want God to deliver you from the fear of man you must be "sincere!" 1 Samuel 16:7 says, "For man looks on the outer appearance, but the Lord looks on the heart."

Action Step #2:
Renew your mind by meditating on the Word of God.

When the Bible speaks of "The Word of God," it means both the Living and the written Word. Jesus Christ is the Living Word, and the Bible is the written Word of God.

God's Word to Joshua is just as applicable for you and me today as it was for him:

> "This book of the law shall not depart from your mouth, but you shall meditate on it day and night, so that you may be careful to do according to all that is written in it; for then you will make your way prosperous, and then you will have success" (Josh. 1:8).

We are to study and meditate on the Word of God, rather than just reading it casually. As you diligently study and think about what God's Word is saying, God will reveal spiritual truth to you by the power of the Holy Spirit. This is how you grow spiritually. What food is to your body, the Bible is to your soul (see Matthew 4:4).

There is no way around it. The better you know the Word of God, the better you know the God of the Word. The better you know God, the stronger His presence becomes in your life. It is the presence and the power of the Holy Spirit abiding in you that enables you to say "No" to the sin that once so easily entangled you. You will become a conqueror and an overcomer through Christ. The better you know your Bible the more useful you are to the Master for spiritual warfare and for counseling others.

> "For the word of God is living and active and sharper than any two-edged sword, and piercing as far as the division of soul and spirit, of both joints and marrow, and able to judge the thoughts and intentions of the heart" (Heb. 4:12).

The Word of God is alive, it is constantly bearing fruit, and it is more effective than any other weapon. What does a sword do? It separates things. And what does the Word of God want to separate you from? The world, the flesh, and the devil. Anytime you see the word *world* in the New Testament, it is a code word for "godlessness." The fashion and the philosophy of the world exert a powerful influence. Its message is all about satisfying the desires of the flesh. Live for the here and now; give no thought to God or the afterlife. The peer pressure from the "everybody's doing it" mentality of the world is like a raging river. The god of this world (Satan) comes to steal, kill and destroy. Here is a verse you should know; it's Rom. 12:2:

> "And do not be conformed to this world, but be transformed by the renewing of your mind, that you may prove what the will of God is, that which is good and acceptable and perfect."

How do you renew your mind? According to Eph. 5:26, you wash it with the water of the Word of God—the Bible. Just as the living Word (Jesus Christ) has power, so the written Word of God also has power. Psalms 119:11 says:

> "I have hidden your word in my heart that I might not sin against you."

Read your Bible until your Bible begins to read you!

Action Step #3:
Know, trust and obey God.

The verse that this book is based on is Prv. 29:25:

"The fear of man brings a snare, but he who trusts in the LORD will be exalted."

The solution to the problem of fearing the creature over the Creator is found in this text. A contrast is drawn between fearing mortal man and trusting the Eternal God. The word *trust* in the original Hebrew means: "to be confident or sure." The same word is used in Ps. 9:10:

"And those who know Thy name will put their trust in Thee; for Thou, O LORD, hast not forsaken those who seek Thee."

In this verse, the Holy Spirit equates knowing God's name with trusting Him. That is exactly what we see in Prv. 29:25. In essence it says, He who trusts in the LORD will be delivered from the fear of man. In Hebrew, the word *LORD* is not a title, but a name. It consists of four consonants YHWH (pronounced *yood hay vav hay* in Hebrew) and no vowels. It represents the most holy and proper name of God. Theologians call it the Tetragrammaton. To the ancient Jews, this name was so revered they dared not even speak it for fear of breaking the third Commandment. As a result, the true pronunciation of YHWH has been lost, but the meaning has not. It literally means, The Eternal, Self-Existent One. YHWH—the God who is, the God who was, and the God who always will be, from eternity past to eternity future, without beginning and without end, the great I AM. God does not change. For God to change He would either have to get better or worse. That is impossible; He is perfect! If you don't know Him, His address is Deut. 4:29.

Action Step #4: Develop an eternal perspective.

If I were to offer you a bucket of diamonds or a bucket of water you wouldn't think twice about which to choose. But if you were crawling in the desert dying from dehydration, and I offered you a bucket of diamonds or a bucket of fresh cold water, the water would mean the difference between life and death. You would take the water! Now imagine your life is over and you are standing before the judgment bar of God, facing eternity. What if you are one of the people who never took time to study the Bible, you 'blew off' church, and never led anyone to Christ? What will be important to you then?

"By faith Moses, when he had grown up, refused to be called the son of Pharaoh's daughter; choosing rather to endure ill-treatment with the people of God than to enjoy the passing pleasures of sin; considering the reproach of Christ greater riches than the treasures of Egypt; for he was looking to the reward" (Heb. 11:24-26).

Living in the light of eternity was a major theme of Jesus' teaching. The twenty-fifth chapter of Matthew is the climax of the Gospels. There we find the sheep and the goats standing before the judgment bar of God:

> "These (goats) shall go away into everlasting punishment, but the righteous (sheep) into life eternal."

Action Step #5: Learn to control your thoughts.

Here is a simple yet powerful spiritual truth. Every sin begins as a thought. James 1:14-15 says:

> "But each one is tempted when he is carried away and enticed by his own lust. Then when lust has conceived, it gives birth to sin; and when sin is completed, it brings forth death."

James explains the process of sin. He says, "Each one is tempted when he is carried away." He is speaking of being carried away in our imaginations. When a sinful idea enters our minds we are being tempted. It is not a sin to be tempted; Jesus was tempted, yet He was without sin. You cross the line from temptation to sin, when you realize what you are contemplating and you continue to *entertain* the thought instead of rejecting it. It is one thing to see a woman; it is another thing to *look with lust.* In Matthew 5:27-28 Jesus said:

> "You have heard that it was said, 'You shall not commit adultery'; but I say to you, that everyone who looks on a woman to lust for her has committed adultery with her already in his heart."

Here is the key to victory over your thought life. It is found in 2 Cor. 10:3-5:

> "For though we walk in the flesh, we do not war according to the flesh, for the weapons of our warfare are not of the flesh, but divinely powerful for the destruction of fortresses. We are destroying speculations and every lofty thing raised

up against the knowledge of God, and we are taking every thought captive to the obedience of Christ."

Here is another liberating spiritual truth, from Phil 4:8-9:

> "Finally, brethren, whatever is true, whatever is honorable, whatever is right, whatever is pure, whatever is lovely, whatever is of good repute, if there is any excellence and if anything worthy of praise, let your mind dwell on these things. The things you have learned and received and heard and seen in me, practice these things; and the God of peace shall be with you."

If what you are thinking does not fit through the grid of this verse, you have no business thinking it. If it is not true, if it is not right, if it is not pure, if it is not lovely, if it is not of good repute, if it is not excellent, if it is not worthy of praise, you need to throw it back. Your mind is not a garbage dump, it's a temple! Here is another great verse. It's Col. 3:2:

> "Set your mind on the things above, not on the things that are on earth. For you have died and your life is hidden with Christ in God. When Christ, who is our life, is revealed, then you also will be revealed with Him in glory."

Action Step #6: Redeem the time.

You know how it is when someone has a baby? The family and friends come over; and they oooo and ahhh over the baby. Well, if you come back in five years and the child is still in the same crib, nobody's going, "Oooo, ahhh, *what a beautiful baby!*" Something is very wrong. The point is, if you have not grown spiritually in the last five years, there is nothing cute about it. If that is the case, it is obvious that you are wasting rather than investing your time.

Have you heard the story of Charles Schwab and Ivy Lee? Schwab was president of Bethlehem Steel and Ivy Lee was a consultant. He was hired by Schwab to show them how to be more productive. The challenge was: "Show me a way to get more things done with my time." Schwab agreed to pay him "anything within reason" if Lee's ideas worked. As incredible as it sounds, this was Lee's recommendation:

"Write down the most important tasks you have to do tomorrow. Number them in order of importance. When you arrive in the morning, begin at once on number one and stay on it until it is completed. Recheck your priorities, then begin with number two. Then number three. Make this a habit every working day. Pass it on to those under you. Try it as long as you like, then send me your check for what you think it's worth."

That one idea turned Bethlehem Steel Corporation into the biggest independent steel producer in the world within five years! How much did Schwab pay his consultant? Several weeks after receiving the note, he sent Lee a check for $25,000, admitting it was the most profitable lesson he had ever learned. That was in 1904, when the average worker in the US was being paid $2 per day!

Here is a wonderful principle for spiritual growth found in Prov. 13:20:

"He who walks with wise men will be wise, but the companion of fools will suffer harm."

Reading great books is one way to walk with wise men. Watch too much TV and you are the companion of a fool. Watching TV is one of the biggest time wasters there is. When you are watching TV, you are saying, in effect, "I don't have anything better to do." Watching TV is not in and of itself a sin, unless the program you are watching is immoral. Sadly, most of what spews out of the electronic idol is unadulterated waste. The real problem of too much TV is the cumulative effect it has on you over months and years.

The enemy of your soul wants to 'dumb you down' and keep you there. The TV is one of the best ways ever devised to do just that. To waste the time and the life God gave you is one of the greatest tragedies of all. Most people are completely oblivious to what is really going on in our world for three reasons:

1. They waste their time watching TV and do not read.

2. They get and accept the "news" from the major networks without seeking outside sources, thinking they are getting balanced, accurate, and unbiased information.

3. They are biblically illiterate.

In Eph. 5:15-17, we read:

> "Therefore be careful how you walk, not as unwise men, but as wise, making the most of your time, because the days are evil. So then do not be foolish, but understand what the will of the Lord is."

When salespeople approach me in supermarkets to ask if I would like to subscribe to the newspaper, I always answer by saying, "No thanks. I read tomorrow's newspaper today." When they ask how that is possible, I tell them I read the Bible. As a general rule, you won't get any smarter watching TV, movies or playing video games. TV is actually an escape from reality. God gave us a manual for successful living, and He expects us to at least know the basics. Why? Because that is the primary way you grow in your relationship with Him, in spiritual wisdom, and in discernment.

God Expects Us To Produce Fruit

Picture a madman throwing $100 bills into the Atlantic Ocean or diamonds overboard into Lake Michigan. This gives you a rough idea of how foolish it is to waste the golden vials of time which your Creator places in your hands every morning. Think about it. Now, in this life on Planet Earth, is the only opportunity you will ever have to store up riches in heaven. You can invest your time or you can waste your time, but once it's gone, you can never get it back. If I could retrieve a day I had lost or had stolen by putting an ad in the newspaper, it might read like this:

> "Lost. One 24 hour, 24 karat golden day, studded with 60 diamond minutes. Each minute studded with 60 ruby seconds. If found, please return to owner."

In Ps. 90:12, God's Word says:

> "So teach us to number our days, that we may present to Thee a heart of wisdom."

Action Step #7: Learn how to present the gospel.

One of the main reasons Christians are afraid to share the Gospel of Jesus Christ is the total inability to explain in a compelling manner why they believe what they believe. Knowing how to present the

Gospel the way God intended it to be done builds spiritual muscle and gives you courage. Most people freely admit that they believe God exists. Our job is to introduce them to the "...one mediator between God and man, the man Christ Jesus" (1 Tim. 2:5).

Fortunately, God did not leave us to fend for ourselves when it comes to presenting the Gospel. He left us a perfect systematic theology of evangelism that cannot be improved upon by man. It consists of three simple points that any intelligent 12-year-old can understand. Remember, these are God's reasons to believe, so they cannot be improved upon.

1. General revelation. The general revelation that God exists is found in creation itself. Romans 1:20 is clear:

   "For since the creation of the world His invisible attributes, His eternal power and divine nature, have been clearly seen, being understood through what has been made, so that they are without excuse."

   Here is general revelation in Psalms 19:1-3:

   "The heavens declare the glory of God; the skies proclaim the work of His hands. Day after day they pour forth speech; night after night they display knowledge. There is no speech or language where their voice is not heard."

   Just as the Mona Lisa is proof positive that there was a Leonardo da Vinci, so creation itself is proof positive that there is a Creator. It's a no-brainer. I told you this was easy!

2. The Word of God—Living and Written. That is Jesus Christ and the Bible. See Col. 1:15-17 and 2 Tim. 3:16.

   It is Bible prophecy that proves beyond the shadow of a doubt that the Scriptures are divinely inspired—proof positive that God exists. "How," you ask? No human being can even come close to predicting the future with 100% accuracy. Only a person with omniscience can do that. That is what makes the Bible the most unique book ever written. Between it and every other so-called "holy book" there is no possible term of comparison. The Bible was written over the course of 1,500 years and on three continents—Europe,

Asia, and Africa. It was written in three languages—Hebrew, Aramaic, and Greek. It was produced by 40 different writers, and yet it has a beginning, middle, and an end. It speaks on hundreds of controversial topics in perfect harmony. Completed more than 2,000 years ago, the Bible tells us how the world began and how it will end, it answers the question of evil, the purpose of man, and the future of the nations politically, militarily, economically, and spiritually. The Word of God plainly states that the nation of Israel plays the major role in the end-time events of human history, all in stunning detail, thousands of years in advance! Using Israel as an object lesson, the main theme of the Bible from beginning to end is how God can forgive man's sin without compromising His justice. From Genesis to Revelation, it is all about the Lord Jesus Christ.

How Miraculous Is The Bible?

Imagine if I predicted 1,000 years in advance the exact city in which the President of the United States would be born, his exact birth date, what nationality he would be, what family he would come from, what kind of car he would drive, where he would go to school, what his name would be, what his father's and mother's names would be, how old he would be when he died, when he would die, how he would die, plus dozens of his most significant accomplishments in specific detail, and I were 100% accurate on every count. Would that be a miracle? That is exactly what the Bible did in reference to Jesus Christ!

According to J. Barton Payne's book, *Encyclopedia of Biblical Prophecy,* there are 8,352 predictive verses in the Bible. According to astrophysicists and qualified American science professors, the odds of 2,500 prophecies being fulfilled by chance alone are 1 with 2,000 zeros after it. That number is more than all of the atoms in the "known" universe. According to mathematicians, if a number has more than 50 zeros after it, the odds of that happening by chance alone are virtually impossible. This is irrefutable proof that the Bible is divinely inspired! For documentation on this, see Peter Stoner's book, *Science Speaks,* published by Moody Press.

3. Conscience and the Moral Law. This is found in Romans 2:15:

> "in that they show the work of the Law written in their hearts, their conscience bearing witness, and their thoughts alternately accusing or else defending them."

The essence of the Ten Commandments is written on every man's heart. Every man knows instinctively it is wrong to murder, it is wrong to steal, it is wrong to lie, it is wrong to have another man's wife. Every man knows there is a God in heaven because the sun, the moon, and the stars declare His glory! When you walk a person gently and lovingly through the Ten Commandments you are showing him or her exactly why they need God's forgiveness through Jesus Christ. Sin is the transgression of the law. It's because we have all broken God's law that we need His forgiveness. If there were no God, there would be no universal moral law.

Action Step #8: Go out and do it.

For many if not for most people, life is empty and basically boring. That's why they sit around watching TV. Glorifying God and advancing the Kingdom are two of the reasons you were created. When you tell someone about Jesus it is a win-win for you, even if he or she rejects God's gift. Here is why. In Luke 6:22-23, Jesus said:

> "Blessed are you when men hate you, and ostracize you, and cast insults at you, and spurn your name as evil, for the sake of the Son of Man. Be glad in that day, and leap for joy, for behold, your reward is great in heaven; for in the same way their fathers used to treat the prophets."

And, in 1 Pet. 4:14 we read:

> "If you are reviled for the name of Christ, you are blessed, because the Spirit of glory and of God rests upon you."

And, in Dan. 12:3 God's Word promises:

> "Those who are wise will shine like the brightness of the heavens, and those who lead many to righteousness, like the stars for ever and ever."

Like I said, you can't lose. Find someone in your church who is involved in real front-line evangelism such as a nursing-home ministry, a jail ministry, or a street-witnessing ministry. Find people who are involved in passing out tracts, or going to the local rescue mission or hospital, and ask if you can go with them. If there is no one in your church who does that, you probably need to find a new church. Short-term mission trips are also life-changing!

When Jesus sent out His disciples to bring the message of salvation to a lost and dying world, He sent them out in pairs. The reason is clear: there is strength and courage in numbers. Here are the words of King Solomon in Eccl. 4:9-12:

> "Two are better than one because they have a good return for their labor. For if either of them falls, the one will lift up his companion. But woe to the one who falls when there is not another to lift him up. Furthermore, if two lie down together they keep warm, but how can one be warm alone? And if one can overpower him who is alone, two can resist him. A cord of three strands is not quickly torn apart."

I have taken hundreds of people with me to the local jail to provide chapel services. It's like a church service, but a lot more personal and informal. Many have asked me just to let them observe, because they don't want to say anything. Well, I understand that most people are afraid of public speaking. However, I'm also aware that if you don't know you are going to be called upon, you don't have the pressure of worrying about what you are going to say. So, in the middle of the service, I'll turn to the person and say something like, "Do you love the Lord?" They always answer in the affirmative, so at that point, I ask, "Would you please tell these men what God has done for you?" Virtually every time I have done this, afterwards, the people were very excited that they spoke up publicly for Jesus, in many cases, for the first time. It is such an exhilarating experience that many have come out of the closet and shut the door behind them.

Find someone who is involved in evangelism and tag along. You'll be glad you did. Each time it gets easier, and it's always a deeply enriching, spiritual experience. Proverbs 11:25 speaks of this principle:

> "The generous man will be prosperous, and he who waters will himself be watered."

Small Group Questions

1. How do we know the Bible is true?

2. When God delivers you from a sinful habit, it's called a work of _____. What is your part?

3. Read Matthew 10:32-33. In what ways do we deny Christ? What does He mean by the second half of that verse?

4. Read Ezek. 22:30-31. What are the implications of this verse?

5. What does *sincere* mean? Why is being sincere important, and how does God know if you are?

6. What does YHWH mean?

7. Do you know God's address? Check Deut. 4:29, Prv. 2:1-5, Mat. 7:7, Jas. 4:8, and Rev. 3:20. What are these verses saying?

8. What are the three main points for sharing the Gospel found in Action Step Seven?

9. According to the author, "Most people are completely oblivious to what is really going on in our world for three reasons." What are they?

10. Go over the 8 action steps on how to be delivered from the fear of man. Which steps are most helpful to you?

CHAPTER NINE

A Still More Excellent Way—
Love Never Fails

—∿∿—

When Jesus began His teaching 2,000 years ago, the Roman Empire ruled the world with an iron fist. They won all their arguments by killing their enemies. The teaching of Jesus could not have been more antithetical. Jesus said, "Love your enemies." The Roman Empire represented the greatest political, military, and the economic power on earth. The church had no political power and no army. It started with twelve men, and one of them was a traitor! The Roman soldiers were armed to the teeth with swords, horses, chariots, and armor. They were the largest army in the world, capable of crushing anything in their path and they did—almost.

Here we are, 2,000 years later. The Roman Empire fell, and the church has more members alive on this day than the total number of people that made up the Empire over its entire 500- year history! The same is true in the animal world. The lions and the tigers are on the endangered species list, but there are plenty of lambs and kittens!

Love is more powerful than the sword. Love can break the hardest hearts when nothing else can. Chapter thirteen of First Corinthians contains what many believe to be the Bible's most noble and magnificent chapter. A diamond among the jewels, it's known as "the love chapter." Its power will never diminish. In Jesus' name I now ask you: do you love your neighbors enough to tell them about Jesus? In 1 Cor. 13:1-8, Paul teaches us how to apply the most powerful force on earth:

> "If I speak with the tongues of men and of angels, but do not have love, I have become a noisy gong or a clanging cymbal. And if I have the gift of prophecy, and know all mysteries and all knowledge; and if I have all faith, so as to remove mountains, but do not have love, I am nothing. And if I give

all my possessions to feed the poor, and if I deliver my body to be burned, but do not have love, it profits me nothing."

Paul says that a loving person is greater than the greatest orator who lacks love. Love is great; words and rhetoric alone mean nothing by comparison. He goes on to say, if you are a prophet without peer, if you understand the secrets and the mysteries of the universe and can explain them so even a child can understand, if the foundation of your life is not love, your insights mean nothing. The most generous philanthropy and even martyrdom mean nothing if the motive is not love.

In the English language we have only one word for love. You can say, "I love spaghetti, I love my dog, and I love my wife." Do you love your wife in the same way you love your dog? In the ancient Greek language of the New Testament, there were four words to express the idea of love.

- *Storge* means affection. It is the word used to describe love for your father, mother, brothers and sisters.
- *Philos* means friendship and fondness.
- *Eros* speaks of the intimate love between a husband and wife.
- *Agape* means unconditional, self-sacrificial love.

Agape love is absolutely unique to Christianity. You will not find this concept in any other religion, philosophy, or system of thought. It means that I love you even if you don't love me back. It was agape that Christ demonstrated on the cross. While He hung there in unspeakable agony, His accusers laughed, mocked, ridiculed, and spat at Him. The soldiers were throwing dice at the foot of the cross to see who would keep His robe. It was in this context that He prayed:

"Father, forgive them for they know not what they do."

No mere man could have done that. This kind of compassion was so antithetical to human nature the thief on His right had the divine realization that Jesus was the Son of God. He got saved right on the spot!

In Matthew 5:46, Jesus said:

"For if you love those who love you, what reward have you? Do not even the tax-gatherers do the same?"

To put this in modern terminology, even the Mafia love their own family members, but they kill their enemies. If you only love those who love you, how are you any different from the Mafia? Love is the distinguishing mark of the Christian.

What Is Love?

First of all, love is not abstract, arbitrary, or relative. When the Bible speaks of love, it is a principled love; it has ethical standards. Because I love my wife and my family, there are certain things I do, and there are certain things I do not do. This is based on God's universal moral law. In Romans 13:8-10, the Holy Spirit uses the words *law* and *love* in the same breath:

> "Owe nothing to anyone except to love one another; for he who loves his neighbor has fulfilled the law. For this, 'You shall not commit adultery, you shall not murder, you shall not steal, you shall not covet,' and if there is any other commandment, it is summed up in this saying, 'you shall love your neighbor as yourself.' Love does no wrong to a neighbor; love therefore is the fulfillment of the law."

If I love my neighbor, I will not lust after his wife, I will not murder him if he angers me, I will not steal from him, I will not lie to him, and I will not be envious of him. Love is defined; it has boundaries; it is not whatever you want it to be. Jesus said, "If you love Me you will obey My commandments." God *is* love, and God defines love.

Love Is Patient

When it comes to personality types, I am a Type A. I admit I don't like waiting for anything and, frankly, I'm wound a little tight. I have been battling this most of my adult life. At 10 a.m. on Sunday morning, if everybody is not in the car ready to go to church, I start getting "a little concerned." If 10:02 rolls around, I'm ready to start honking the horn. If we are not on the road by 10:05, I start losing my sanctification!

Love Is Kind

Kindness is proactive. When Jesus said, "Love your neighbor," the question was asked, "Who is my neighbor?" Jesus told the story of the Good Samaritan. Kindness has been defined as:

> "An unselfish concern for the welfare of others."

Did you know that 80% of the people who are put in nursing homes in America never see their family members again? In light of Matthew 25:31-46, I fear for those who are guilty of this sin.

One Kind Word Can Change A Life

I remember reading a story by R.C. Sproul. While he was a seminary professor, one of his students who happened to be a paraplegic asked for prayer after class one day. R.C. asked about his need and offered up a simple heart-felt prayer. In his prayer he included the words, "And, Lord, please be merciful to this man." When the professor looked up, there were tears streaming down the student's face. When R.C. gently asked why he was crying the young man replied, "No one ever called me a *man* before." Love is kind, and one kind word can change a life!

Love Is Not Jealous

Two of the greatest preachers in history were Charles Haddon Spurgeon and D.L. Moody. As contemporaries in the 19th century, Spurgeon was to England what Moody was to America. But intellectually and theologically, they were worlds apart. While neither man had any formal theological training, Spurgeon was a wordsmith and a genius. He had a vocabulary of 25,000 words and is still considered one of the greatest orators and most prolific writers in church history. Moody on the other hand, had very poor command of the English language—his grammar was atrocious. Theologically, Spurgeon was a strict Calvinist and Moody was a committed Arminian. Spurgeon never gave altar calls after his sermons and Moody always gave an altar call. Yet both men were used mightily of God.

Moody was invited to Europe to preach a number of evangelistic outreaches. When he came to London, Spurgeon graciously invited him to preach at his 6,000-member Metropolitan Tabernacle. Spurgeon set aside their theological differences and graciously told Moody that he was free to give an altar call in his church.

Many of us can learn a valuable lesson from these two men. Here is what Spurgeon said in his book *Lectures To My Students* about bringing in guest speakers to your church:

"To call in another brother every now and then to take the lead in evangelistic services will be found very wise and useful; for there are some fish that never will be taken in your net, but will surely fall to the lot of another fisherman. Fresh voices penetrate where the accustomed sound has lost effect, and they tend also to beget a deeper interest in those already attentive. Sound and prudent evangelists may lend help even to the most efficient pastor, and gather in fruit which he has failed to reach; at any rate it makes a break in the continuity of ordinary services, and renders them less likely to become monotonous. Never suffer jealousy to hinder you in this. Suppose another lamp should outshine yours, what will it matter so long as it brings light to those whose welfare you are seeking? Say with Moses, 'Would God all the Lord's servants were prophets.' He who is free from selfish jealousy will find that no occasion will suggest it; his people may be well aware that their pastor is excelled by others in talent, but they will be ready to assert that he is surpassed by none in love to their souls. It is not needful for a loving son to believe that his father is the most learned man in the parish; he loves him for his own sake, and not because he is superior to others. Call in every now and then a warm-hearted neighbor, utilize the talent in the church itself, and procure the services of some eminent soul-winner, and this may, in God's hands, break up the hard soil for you, and bring you brighter days."

Love Does Not Brag And Is Not Arrogant

Arrogance and boasting are manifestations of pride. We do well to remember that "God resists the proud, but gives grace to the humble." In John 15:5, Jesus said:

"I am the vine, you are the branches; he who abides in Me, and I in him, he bears much fruit; for apart from Me you can do nothing."

We draw our lives from Christ. What do you have that you have not received from Him? He is the source of life. As one preacher said, "God will use anybody, as long as they don't want to touch the glory." Like Paul, our boast is in the cross.

Love Does Not Act Unbecomingly

I love a story George Sweeting tells: a father was driving his son to school one morning and apparently not everyone else on the road met his expectations for a smooth driving experience. Later the same day, the boy was driving with his mother running some errands. The boy said, "Mom, where do all the idiots live?" The mother somewhat surprised replied, "What do you mean?" The boy said, "Well, when Dad drove me to school this morning, we saw seven idiots!" Children do not always listen to what we say, but they imitate us perfectly. Love does not act unbecomingly.

Love Does Not Seek Its Own

Love means not always insisting on your own way. Remember, when you're always right, you're wrong! What would happen to our relationships if we all followed Paul's admonition in Philippians to "Consider other people more important than ourselves?" Selfishness is the essence of sin. We would do well to remember the last words of Paul as he left the elders at Ephesus, "Remember the words of the Master Himself, 'It is more blessed to give than to receive.'"

Love Is Not Provoked; It Keeps No Record Of Wrongs

Today we have things like road rage. I remember reading about an incident in California where two men got into an argument and one ended up shooting the other to death with a bow and arrow! Love, rather than becoming angry when suffering a wrong, chooses to forgive. If you keep a list of all the wrong things people have done to you, throw it away along with the one that records all the wrongs you have accumulated over the years. Here is a life-changing truth from Prv. 17:9:

> "He who covers a transgression seeks love, but he who repeats a matter separates intimate friends."

Love Does Not Rejoice In Unrighteousness, But Rejoices With The Truth

There is a certain mean streak in human nature that enjoys seeing others suffer. Love takes no pleasure in other people's misfortune, even your enemies. Love has no greater joy than to see someone walking in truth. God's will for us is to "do justly, to love mercy, and to walk in humility" (Micah 6:8).

Love Bears All Things, Believes All Things, Hopes All Things, Endures All Things

Loves bears all things including, but not limited to, insults, failures, loss of life, limb, etc., without complaining or blaming others. The word *bears* could also be translated "covers." Love covers a multitude of sin, rather than gossiping or needlessly exposing them. Love gives people the benefit of the doubt, rather than assuming the worst. Loves never gives up hope.

Love Never Fails

In 1 Cor. 13:13, Paul said: "But now abide faith, hope, love, these three; but the greatest of these is love." Somebody once said, "The opposite of love is not hate, it's selfishness."

"For God so **loved** the world, that He **gave**" John. 3:16.

When the Bible says, "love is patient and love is kind," I confess to you, I fall short. By this standard, we all do. I have news for you. Christianity isn't difficult; it's impossible. Nobody can live up to this standard; that is why we need a Savior! When you read the 'love' chapter, you can insert the name Jesus before each of the attributes of love, and it fits perfectly. "Love is the manifestation of the divine life."[1]

A Life-Changing Illustration

A lady was driving to church on a cold, winter Sunday morning. On her way she stopped for a red light. Just after the light turned green, her car stalled in the middle of the intersection. As she tried to re-start the car, the man behind her laid on his horn. As she attempted to start the car again, she noticed in her rearview mirror the man behind her getting out of his car. He walked right up to her window, bent down and started yelling at her to move her car, He was late for a very important appointment! With her hands shaking, she tried it again, and much to her relief, the car started. Arriving at church she was still visibly shaken by the man's anger. After the musical portion of the service, it was announced, "We have a guest speaker today!" After giving him a grand introduction about how qualified he was and what a wonderful man of God he was, as he was walking up to the pulpit, you guessed it, it was him! This lady was aghast! She stood to her feet, turned around, and walked out. She had no interest in hearing a word this man had to say, and rightly so.

Love is the greatest virtue and the most powerful force on earth. Love is greater than academic achievement, economic influence, or political power. In the end, the nations will fail. Jesus Christ and His church will stand forever. The fear of man is based on pride. Pride is self-centered and, therefore, antithetical to love. You can never be all that God intended you to be as long as you love the praise of man more than the praise that comes from the only God. If you need more love, become more loving. The only question remaining is, do you love your brother enough to tell him the truth about Jesus?

My Testimony

I "believed" in Jesus when I was fifteen years old. I "believed" so strongly, I "believed" I would have died for Jesus rather than renounce my faith. My problem was, I wasn't living for Him. I realize now that ours is not the "god of the dead; He is the God of the living" (Mk. 12:27). He didn't want me to die for Him (necessarily), He wanted me to live for Him. He's not looking for dead sacrifices anymore; He's looking for live ones. Some people do call me a "Jesus Freak," and some people do think I'm a "religious fanatic," but God calls me "son"!

The End

Small Group Questions

1. What was most meaningful to you in this chapter?

2. What is meant by "God's love is principled love"?

3. How do law and love relate to each other?

4. What does Paul mean when he says, "Love never fails"?

5. Read Micah 6:8. What areas of your life do you need to change to conform to God's will in this verse?

6. How does a lack of love affect your credibility? Why?

7. Read each of the attributes of love out loud and ask, "What are some practical ways we can apply these definitions of love in our daily lives?

8. Compare yourself to the measure of love found in 1 Cor. 13. In this light, why is pride so sinful?

9. What is the difference between lust and love?

10. If you only had six months to live, what would you do differently? What guarantee do you have of living another six months?

Appendix 1

Where Did God Come From?

Try to imagine nothing exists. No earth, sun, moon, stars, or galaxies. There are no elements such as carbon, hydrogen, nitrogen, or oxygen. No such things as time, space, or matter. No universe, no God—nothing! How do you define *nothing*? Aristotle defined it this way,

> "Nothing is what rocks dream about."

If there ever was a time when nothing but nothing existed, then what would exist today? Nothing! Since we know that nothing comes from nothing, we are forced to the inescapable conclusion that, "If anything now exists, either something is eternal, or no one, plus nothing, equals everything."[1]

Amazingly, there is one thing that all scientists, philosophers, and theologians agree on:

> You only have two choices: either God is eternal and uncreated, or matter is eternal and uncreated. There is no third choice.

Steven Hawking, beyond question, is one of the greatest scientific minds since Albert Einstein. He speaks with authority when he says:

> "Today, virtually everyone agrees that the universe and time itself had a beginning."[2]

If the universe had a beginning, then something, or someone, caused it to begin. According to the 2nd law of thermodynamics, the expanding universe, and Einstein's Theory of Relativity, the universe of time, space, and matter (which is energy) had a beginning. Interestingly, this fits the biblical model perfectly. The very first verse in the Bible says:

> "In the beginning God created the heavens and the earth."

In the beginning (that's time), God created (that's energy) the heavens (that's space) and the earth (that's matter). Coincidence?

Imagine that time never ends. If time goes on forever, then there would be no such thing as the last day. Now, reverse the idea. Suppose time went backwards indefinitely, so there was no first day. If time just kept going backwards with no first day, then this day (today) could never arrive! But, this day (today) is here. Therefore, there had to be a first day, and that was the day time began.

Asking The Wrong Question Can Never Produce The Right Answer

Since we know that the universe and time itself had a beginning, that leaves us with our only other option—God is eternal. That being the case, asking, "Where did God come from?" is a nonsensical question. It makes the false assumption that God was created or had a beginning, and then asks, "How is that possible?" The question itself is *fatally flawed*. It is like asking, "Where did the bachelor get his wife?" Or, "What does blue sound like?" Bachelors by definition do not have wives, and colors are not in the category of sound. In exactly the same sense, God is not in the category of created things. So, as Norm Giesler suggests:

> "A better question to begin with is, why is there something rather than nothing?"[3]

> "It was 100 years ago that Albert Einstein published three papers that rocked the world. His papers proved the existence of the atom, introduced the theory of relativity, and described quantum mechanics. His equations for relativity indicated that the universe was expanding. This bothered him because, if it were expanding, it must have had a beginning and a beginner."[4]

Albert Einstein wrote in his book *The World As I See It:*

> "The harmony of natural law reveals an intelligence of such superiority that, compared with it, all the systematic thinking and acting of human beings is an utterly insignificant reflection."

He went on to say:

> "Everyone who is seriously involved in the pursuit of science becomes convinced that a spirit is manifest in the laws

of the Universe—a spirit vastly superior to that of man, and one in the face of which we with our modest powers must feel humble."[5]

In other words, every unbiased scientist must admit that the universe reveals an intelligence so far superior to that of man, it is altogether incomprehensible!

Ron Rhodes put it this way:

> "Since the universe reveals time, space, and matter, sound reasoning demands that there must be a first cause outside of time, space, and matter. Therefore, we must conclude that the first cause is timeless and eternal. We must also conclude that the first cause is immaterial since it transcends space."[6]

> "To have created the universe, in all of its incredible vastness, out of nothing, the First Cause must be omnipotent. To have created the universe with such precision and intricate design, perfect for the existence of human life on earth, the First Cause must be omniscient. To have made an unending series of design choices requires that the First Cause be personal, for an inanimate, impersonal thing cannot make choices. God's personality is also evidenced in the fact that He created personal human beings."[7]

It is far more rational to believe that an intelligent designer created our world than to believe that life, as complex and orderly as it is, came from nothing and assembled itself by random chance. To believe that life as we know it is the product of blind chance is like believing that a monkey could, by pushing the keys on a typewriter, accidentally produce a complete set of encyclopedias without any mistakes in grammar, spelling, punctuation, or sentence structure, and have all the information on world history correct!

Consider Our Solar System

Our Sun is actually a star. It's 93 million miles from earth. It is so large, you could put more than one million earths inside. The temperature of the sun is estimated to be 27 million degrees Fahrenheit at the core. It consumes 400 million tons of hydrogen per second. If you were to buy the energy that one square yard of the sun produces in just one day, at one penny per kilowatt, and if you paid the bill in silver dollars, you would need enough silver dollars to cover the entire United States 4 miles high!

It is the consumption of nuclear fuel that causes the sun to produce light and heat. As it consumes hydrogen, the sun is slowly decreasing in size. This is proof positive that the sun could not have existed from eternity past.

The sun is 26,000 light-years from the center of our Milky Way Galaxy. The galaxy itself is 100,000 light-years across, and 10,000 light-years in diameter at the center. Traveling at the speed of light (186,000 miles per second), it would take you 100,000 years to travel from one end of the Milky Way Galaxy to the other. If you made the trip in a commercial airliner, it would take you billions of years!

Our entire solar system revolves around the center of the Milky Way Galaxy once every 250 million years at a traveling velocity of 558,000 miles per hour. Compared to earth, the sun is huge. But, compared to other stars, our sun is classified by astronomers as a "yellow dwarf." A star named Antares (a red super giant) could hold 64 million of our suns. The largest known star, Epsilon, is so large that if it were placed in the middle of our solar system it would engulf all the planets and moons out to Pluto!

There are 100 billion stars in our galaxy. Multiply this number by another 100 billion (the estimated number of galaxies in the known universe). If each galaxy contains 100 billion stars, we could expect the existence of 10,000 billion, billion stars in the known universe!

The question any thinking person must ask is, where did it all come from? What is the source of power and wisdom that causes the earth to rotate while it revolves around the sun at just the right speed and at just the right distance? What holds it in place? What causes the entire solar system to rotate around the center of the Milky Way Galaxy once every 250 million years? And, how is it those 100 billion stars all stay in place, marching like soldiers as the whole system revolves?

"Our limited minds cannot grasp the mysterious force that moves the constellations." —Albert Einstein

The Earth

"The earth's size and corresponding gravity holds a thin layer of mostly nitrogen and oxygen gases, only extending about 50 miles above the earth's surface. If earth were smaller, an atmosphere would be impossible, like the planet Mercury. If Earth were larger, its atmosphere would contain free hydrogen, like Jupiter. Earth is the only known planet equipped with an atmosphere of the right mixture of gases to sustain plant, animal and human life.

"The Earth is located the right distance from the sun. Consider the temperature swings we encounter, roughly -30 degrees to +120 degrees. If the Earth were any further away from the sun, we would all freeze. Any closer and we would burn up. Even a fractional variance in the Earth's position to the sun would make life on Earth impossible. The Earth remains the perfect distance from the sun while it rotates around the sun at a speed of nearly 67,000 mph. It is also rotating on its axis, allowing the entire surface of the Earth to be properly warmed and cooled every day."[8]

"And our moon is the perfect size and distance from the Earth for its gravitational pull. The moon creates important ocean tides and movement so ocean waters do not stagnate, and yet our massive oceans are restrained from spilling over across the continents."[9]

Water

"Ninety-seven percent of the Earth's water is in the oceans. But on our Earth, there is a system designed which removes salt from the water and then distributes that water throughout the globe. Evaporation takes the ocean waters, leaving the salt, and forms clouds which are easily moved by the wind to disperse water over the land, for vegetation, animals and people. It is a system of purification and supply that sustains life on this planet, a system of recycled and reused water."[10]

The Brain

The human brain weighs about 3 lbs. It is made up of 6 trillion cells. One hundred billion neurons send electrochemical signals to other neurons. Neurophysiologists tell us that the brain has 1 billion long nerve cells that each communicate with 10,000 other cells. That means the brain sends and receives messages between 10,000 billion electrical connections instantaneously. That is more than all the super-computers and communications systems in the world combined. And it all runs on bread and water!

The Eye

The retina in the eye contains 137 million light-sensitive cells that translate everything you see instantaneously through your nervous system, and your brain sees!

> "The greatest scientists have been struck by how strange this is. There is no logical necessity for a universe that obeys rules, let alone one that abides by the rules of mathematics. This astonishment springs from the recognition that the universe doesn't have to behave this way. It is easy to imagine a universe in which conditions change unpredictably from instant to instant, or even a universe in which things pop in and out of existence."[11]

DNA

> "All instruction, all teaching, and all training come with intent. Someone who writes an instruction manual does so with purpose. Did you know that in every cell of our bodies there exists a very detailed instruction code, much like a miniature computer program? As you may know, a computer program is made up of ones and zeros, like this: 110010101011000. The way they are arranged tells the computer program what to do. The DNA code in each of our cells is very similar. It's made up of four chemicals that scientists abbreviate as A, T, G, and C. These are arranged in the human cell like this: CGTGTGACTCGCTCCTGAT and so on. There are three billion of these letters in every human cell. Well, just like you can program your phone to

beep for specific reasons, DNA instructs the cell. DNA is a three-billion-lettered program telling the cell to act in a certain way. It is a full instruction manual." [12]

How Do You Spell H-Y-P-O-C-R-I-T-E?

For more than 50 years, scientists from the S.E.T.I. program (Search for Extraterrestrial Intelligence) have been using radiotelescopes to send out radio signals across the universe, hoping to receive radio transmissions back. If these scientists ever received a radio signal with a pattern as simple as the musical notes from the children's song:

"Twinkle, twinkle little star, how I wonder what you are,"

they would unashamedly, unabashedly, without fear or reservation, hold a press conference and proudly announce to the world that they had positively identified intelligent life in outer space! A repeated pattern that simple, coming from something or someone they had never seen, would rule out random chance because that pattern requires intelligence.

Yet these same scientists can look at the pattern found in a cell's DNA, knowing that within every cell there is a code with three billion bits of information that not only determine your genetic makeup, but continually *instruct* your cell's behavior, then turn around and deny that this is the result of an intelligent designer! I guess it's okay if it's an extraterrestrial, but not the God of the Bible, because He has moral standards, and He holds us accountable. That is the part they don't like.

God Doesn't Believe In Atheists!

It helps to know that everybody actually does believe in God. Well, what about people like Richard Dawkins, Christopher Hitchins, and other so-called "atheists"? Here is God's position in living black and white:

"For the wrath of God is revealed from heaven against all ungodliness and unrighteousness of men, who suppress the truth in unrighteousness, because that which is known about God is evident within them; for God made it evident to them.

"For since the creation of the world His invisible attributes, His eternal power and divine nature, have been clearly seen, being understood through what has been made, so that they are without excuse.

"For even though they knew God, they did not honor Him as God, or give thanks; but they became futile in their speculations, and their foolish heart was darkened.

"For they exchanged the truth of God for a lie, and worshiped and served the creature rather than the Creator, who is blessed forever. Amen" Rom. 1:18-25.

God is saying that no man will stand before Him with any excuse for ignoring or denying His existence. Psalm 14:1 says: "Only the fool says in his heart, 'There is no god.' They are corrupt, they have committed abominable deeds…"

God's logic is so simple a child can understand it. If you see a painting, such as the Mona Lisa, that is irrefutable proof that there is a painter who is at least as gifted as Leonardo da Vinci. Only an irrational or dishonest person would not agree. In Isaiah 1:3 God says:

"Even an ox knows its owner, and a donkey its master's manger."

In other words, since even an animal knows its owner, how much more does a man, made in the image of God, know the God who created him, by looking at creation?

The Hitchhiker

I picked up a hitchhiker around 6:30 p.m. on a Wednesday night on the Eisenhower Expressway going into Chicago. I was on my way to the Cook County Jail with some friends to provide a chapel service. The man got in my van and said, "God bless you. God bless you." I said, "God bless you, too." He said, "Are you into religion?" I said, "No. Are you?" He said, "No!" He asked, "Then why did you say God bless you?" I replied, "Because you said it first!" "Oh, ya." I asked, "So, you don't believe in God?" He said, "Nahh." We just happened to be driving past a huge cemetery on the right, and I asked him, "So, what happened to all those people in that cemetery?" "Oh, I don't know. They're just floatin' around somewhere." I looked back at him; I'm driving 55 mph down the expressway and said, "I know you believe in God. You know you believe in God, and God knows you believe in God. Isn't that right?" He said, "Well, ya." I said, "Good. Now we can talk." My point is, "everybody believes in God." Those who deny this live in denial.

Small Group Questions

1. How would you summarize this chapter?

2. What is the proof that there is a Creator?

3. How does Einstein's Theory of Relativity relate to Genesis 1:1?

4. What was most meaningful to you in this chapter?

5. How does this statement show the eternal nature of God? "If anything now exists, either something is eternal, or nobody, plus nothing, equals everything."

6. How does this chapter help you explain the reality of God?

7. Read Isaiah 1:3. What is God's implication in that statement?

8. How would you paraphrase Romans 1:20?

9. How often does the solar system revolve around the center of the Milky Way Galaxy, and at what speed?

10. What did you think when you read Einstein's quote about this phenomenon?

11. Is it rational to believe that everything could have come from nothing? Why?

12. Why is the question, "Where did God come from?" a nonsensical question?

Appendix 2

If God Is God And God Is Good, Why Is There Evil?

If God is really there, why doesn't He just appear on the ten o'clock news tonight and clear up all of this confusion? That is a great question and, when you know the answer, it's immensely helpful in understanding why the world is like it is. By the way, as for God appearing on the ten o'clock news, He's already done that once back in Exodus chapter 20. They soon forgot the whole incident, and went right back to being hard-hearted and short-sighted.

The number-one excuse people use to justify not believing in God is the question of evil. If God is God, and God is good, why doesn't He remove all the evil people? It is a good thing He doesn't. If God removed all the evil people using His perfect standard, none of us would still be here, and that includes you!

Nevertheless, the question of evil is a legitimate question that deserves an answer, and the Bible provides it. The reason this chapter is included in this book is huge. When you understand why the world is like it is, and you know how it's going to end, you can live with the proper perspective on life. That includes putting God and man in their proper roles.

The answer to the question of evil only makes sense when we see it in the light of the cosmic struggle that has been raging for untold thousands of years between the forces of darkness and the Prince of Peace. It began not in the Garden of Eden, but in Heaven. In Ezek. 28:12, God reveals the mystery of iniquity and allows us to see exactly what happened before time began.

> "Thus says the Lord, 'You had the seal of perfection, full of wisdom and perfect in beauty. You were in Eden, the garden of God; every precious stone adorned you. Your settings and mountings were made of gold; on the day you were created they were prepared. You were anointed as a guardian

cherub, for so I ordained you. You were on the holy mount of God; you walked among the fiery stones.

"You were blameless in your ways from the day you were created, until unrighteousness was found in you. By the abundance of your trade you were internally filled with violence, and you sinned; therefore I have cast you as profane from the mountain of God.

"And I have destroyed you, O covering cherub, from the midst of the stones of fire. Your heart was lifted up because of your beauty; you corrupted your wisdom by reason of your splendor."

When God created the angels, He created one who was "full of wisdom and perfect in beauty." He was known as the "anointed cherub." I don't know about you, but I have never seen an angel. I do know, however, that they are *not* Caucasian females with long blonde hair, nor are they little babies with wings. According to the Bible, angels are extremely powerful creatures capable of performing feats of strength far beyond the ability of any mortal. In 2 Kings chapter 19, we read the account of an angel that slew 185,000 men from the Assyrian army in one night!

In the Garden of Gethsemane, Jesus said He could have called legions of angels (Mat. 26:53), which would have been enough to destroy the entire Roman army in one day. The real battle, however, is "not against flesh and blood, but against the rulers, against the powers, against the world forces of this darkness, against the spiritual forces of wickedness in the heavenly places" (Eph. 6:12).

To get more on the story of what happened with Lucifer, we turn to the prophet Isaiah, written 750 years before Christ came to earth. In Isa. 14:12-14 we read:

"How you have fallen from heaven, O star of the morning, son of the dawn! You have been cut down to the earth, you who have weakened the nations! But you said in your heart, 'I will ascend to heaven; I will raise my throne above the stars of God, and I will sit on the mount of assembly in the recesses of the north. I will ascend above the heights of the clouds; I will make myself like the Most High.'"

There you have it. The first sin in the universe—covetousness. Lucifer became discontented as the "guardian cherub;" he wanted to be worshipped! It was then that his name was changed from Lucifer (which means the light one) to Satan (which means the adversary).

The Rebellion In Heaven

It is believed (based on Rev. 12:4), that Lucifer convinced one third of the angels to follow him instead of God. So, one third of the angels are in opposition to God. The question is, what should He do about it? Look at His options. He could have vaporized them instantaneously. He could have crushed the rebellion with a word! The problem with that approach would be obvious. If the Creator had simply wiped out the fallen angels, the worship in Heaven would have been tainted by fear. We are assured in 1 Jn. 4:18-19 that:

> "There is no fear in love; but perfect love casts out fear, because fear involves punishment, and the one who fears is not perfected in love. We love Him, because He first loved us."

Even though God is sovereign, one thing He cannot do is to make someone love Him. Forced love is a contradiction in terms. If God were to violate your free will here, true love would no longer be possible. So, God said, in effect, "I will prove My love, not with a show of force, but with a demonstration of perfect love." That is where we come in. We are "Exhibit A" to all the host of heaven that *God is love*.

> "God so loved the world, that He gave His only begotten Son, that whoever believes in Him should not perish, but have eternal life." John. 3:16

God Is Testing Us

A close look at what happened in the Garden of Eden is most revealing. God created a small planet and set up a test for all to see. Man was placed in a perfect environment. Adam and Eve were created with a conscience and a free will, and without sin. In Genesis 2, the Lord God gave them everything they needed to live in abundance. He provided Adam with a beautiful helpmate and told them to "Be fruitful and multiply." He said, "From any tree of the garden you may eat freely." As He was about to leave them alone for their honeymoon (my paraphrased version), He turned around and said, "Oh, by the way, there is one thing; just don't eat from the tree of the knowledge of good and evil, for in the day that you eat from it you shall surely die. Have a great day."

When the Lord forbade them to eat from the tree of the knowledge of good and evil, they were then put in the position where good was not the only thing they could do. The choice to obey or disobey was now present in order for man to be morally tested. All the angels in heaven were and are watching God's plan of redemption unfold in real time. So, what happened? In Gen. 3:

> "They both took from its fruit and ate; then the eyes of both
> of them were opened, and they knew that they were naked."

They chose to disobey God and as a result the whole earth was under the curse of sin. Question: Didn't God know that all this would happen beforehand? The answer is, of course! That is why Rev. 13:8 says that Jesus is "the Lamb (was) slain from (before) the foundation of the world."

God is going to let sin run its course. He is going to allow man to rule his own life in order to show what happens when God is excluded from that plan. The New Testament teaches that there will be a war that will end all wars—the war of Armageddon. And, just before this planet is completely destroyed, God is going to stop it. Jesus said, "Unless those days were cut short, no flesh would be saved" (Mat. 24:22). So, when it is all said and done, there will never be another rebellion in heaven. No one will ever question God's wisdom, integrity, ability to rule the universe, His motives, or His love ever again!

The staggering truth is that even the angels who have spent their entire existence in the presence of God are amazed at what a mortal man will do to please the God he has never seen! "In the same way, I tell you, there is joy in the presence of the angels of God over one sinner who repents" (Luke 15:10). Can you imagine how God feels when His people praise Him in church, and pray to Him in the secret closet of prayer (i.e., when no one is looking)?

Imagine a young man driving up to an unmanned toll booth at three o'clock in the morning. The toll is 40 cents, and all he has are two quarters. He is thinking about pulling away without paying just as he sees a police car pull up right behind him! Will he put in the money? Of course. The test comes when he thinks no one is looking. The quality of a man's religion is what he does when he thinks no one is watching.

"You may think you're getting away with something, but I guarantee, there is at least one other person who knows."
—Ravi Zacharias

Small Group Questions

1. What do you believe was the most valuable lesson in this book?

2. Who is responsible for all of the evil in this world?

3. How does understanding evil help you to deal with it?

4. Why can't God force someone to love Him?

5. If God knows everything, why does He test us?

6. Why is God allowing sin to run its course?

7. What are some of the ways a man's true character is revealed? Here are some suggestions: what makes him laugh or cry, how he accepts praise, criticism, wins, loses, spends money, what he does when alone, etc.

8. What answer can you give if someone asks you, "If God is good, why is there evil?"

9. What do we mean by saying the world, the flesh and the devil are your enemies? In what ways do they fight against you?

10. What do you think God is telling you in this book?

End Notes

Chapter 1: The Christians Are Here—Call Out the Lions

[1] The Back to God Hour - Primary Focus. *Back to the Streets.*

[2] A.W. Tozer, *The Knowledge of the Holy,* ch.1. Why we must think rightly about God.

[3] Deut. 20:6-8, 24:5.

Chapter 2: The Greatest Demonstration of Power Anyone Has Ever Seen

[1] The video *Discovering the Real Mt. Sinai* is availble from the BASE Institute, Palmer Lake, CO.

[2] This chapter was adapted from, Philip DelRe: *Jesus Christ the Master Evangelist: How to Present the Gospel the Way Jesus Did* (Belvidere: Voice Publishing, 2004), p. 1.

[3] *I Have a Dream.* A speech given on Aug. 28, 1963 by Martin Luther King during the March on Washington.

Chapter 5: The Righteous Are Bold as Lions

[1] Nancy Leigh DeMoss, *Revive Our Hearts* Radio program. *Faith Produces Faithfulness,* 9-30-09.

Chapter 6: The Amazing Spiritual Secrets of Salt and Light

I borrowed the outline for salt and a couple of the illustrations from an old audio sermon by the late great Adrian Rogers.

[1] I am indebted to Lakita Garth for this excellent illustration on purity.

Chapter 7: There Are Two Kinds Of People In The World: Those Who Think They Can, And Those Who Think They Can't, And They're Both Right

[1] *The International Standard Bible Encyclopedia* (Grand Rapids: WM. B. Eerdmans Publishing Co., 1939) Vol. 3, p. 1439.

Chapter 10: A Still More Excellent Way—Love Never Fails

[1] H.A. Ironside, *1 Corinthians* (New Jersey: Loizeaux Brothers, Inc, 1938) p. 432.

[2] I am indebted to Dr. David Larsen for his life-changing message on 1 Cor. 13. It was given at the Maywood Evangelical Free Church in Rockford, Illinois, on May 17, 2009. His message inspired me to write my own sermon on this text. Some of the ideas in this chapter were adapted from his excellent exposition.

Dr. Larsen is the Professor of Preaching Emeritus at Trinity Evangelical Divinity School in Deerfield, IL and is one of America's finest biblical expositors.

Appendix 1: Where Did God Come From?

[1] *Does God Exist?* Audio-taped sermon from the late, great Dr. Walter Martin, the original "Bible Answer Man" and author of *The Kingdom Of The Cults.*

[2] Norman Geisler, *I Don't Have Enough Faith to Be an Atheist.* (Wheaton, IL. Crossway 2004).

[3] Ibid.

[4] Perry Marshall, "*Where Did God Come From*?" Cosmicfingerprints.com

[5] This essay by Albert Einstein was originally published in "Forum and Century," vol. 84, pp. 193-194, the thirteenth in the Forum series, *Living Philosophies.* It is also included in *Living Philosophies* (pp. 3-7) New York: Simon & Schuster, 1931.

[6] Ron Rhodes, *Answering the Objections of Atheists, Agnostics, & Skeptics.* Eugene, Oregon. Harvest House 2006, p. 56.

[7] Ibid.

[8] R.E.D. Clark, Creation (Lyndon: Tyndale Press, 1946), p. 20. As quoted in: *Answering Atheism With Questions* by Philip DelRe. Published by Voice Publishing.

[9] Ibid.

[10] *The Wonders of God's Creation*, Moody Institute of Science (Chicago, IL).

[11] Dinesh D'Souza, *What's So Great About Christianity*? (Regnery Publishing, Inc. 2007).

[12] Francis S. Collins, director of the Human Genome Project and author of *The Language of God* (Free Press, New York, NY), 2006.

Appendix 2: If God is God and God is Good, Why is There Evil?

[1] This chapter was adapted from: Philip DelRe: *Jesus Christ the Master Evangelist: How to Present the Gospel the Way Jesus Did.* (Belvidere, Il: Voice Publishing, 2004), p. 79.